MW00577372

BETTER THAN I FOUND IT

Stories of Patient Experience and Healthcare Leadership

KATHERINE KALTHOFF, CPXP

TABLE OF CONTENTS

FOREWORD

I first met Kate in 2016 when she connected with me on LinkedIn. She was living in Chicago and planning a move to Lake Tahoe in the coming months. I was the Director of Patient Experience at Renown Health in Reno and Kate was looking for a job to come to when she and her family arrived out west. I didn't have an opening at that point, but something about her told me I had to find a way to get her on my team.

Kate and I spoke several times and met to discuss her previous work experience. Kate had just the qualities I wanted: extensive experience in the field of patient experience, insight into innovative change management, and passion for people and her work. Not to mention, just an all-around fun person to spend time with!

I began my healthcare career as an ICU nurse in Chicago and had previously served as a Studer Coach and as an Advisor with Press Ganey. There were a lot of great things happening at Renown, so when one of my staff moved to a management role in another part of the organization, I immediately worked to get Kate on our team.

In the time we worked together, Kate brought a perspective we hadn't seen before. She had a way of looking at things and presenting ideas to front line staff in such a way that made it relatable and easy to understand. The nurses, leaders and physicians all really appreciated her fresh approach to improving both the employees and patient's experiences.

I've been reading Kate's blog, iamthepatientexperience.net, since Kate began writing, and I always looked forward to each moving story and the message it contains. She never fails to capture a real life story that everyone can relate to and learn from. Her style of writing is just the way she speaks – in an honest, warm, knowledgeable, and often very funny manner. It is with great pleasure that I write this forward to Kate's collection of work. I know you'll enjoy it every bit as much as I did, and perhaps see situations you encounter every day in a whole new light, as I do from listening to, working with and reading Kate's blogs.

Lorna Tirman, Ph.D., MHA, B.S., R.N., CPXP

INTRODUCTION

I didn't set out to write a book.

I'd been talking to a friend of mine about everything I was trying to do as a new manager of a patient experience program, telling him all about my wins as well as my frustrations. He was interested in hearing the behind-the-scenes stories; he'd become all too familiar with doctors and hospitals after his wife had a stroke a few years earlier. She was young, healthy, and took great care of herself so it was a complete surprise when he suddenly became the caregiver of a woman who lost just about all function of her left side.

So when I told him I was working hard to build a culture of compassion and service in this very large physician group, he wanted to hear all about it and share some of his less than pleasant experiences. We spoke almost daily about what needed fixing in healthcare, and one day he told me I should write a blog. To say I resisted is an understatement.

It took a while, but after a few months, I finally decided to give it a try. I started a website, got some design help and started writing. From my time in organ transplant in Chicago, a move to

Sacramento, then to my present role here in Texas, these are my experiences, observations, approaches, and results as chronicled at iamthepatientexperience.net.

Each of the entries stands on its own, so you can jump around to any section or chapter you'd like but as you read them, I think you'll see how they all tie together.

I've had the privilege of working with some incredible people; inspiring leaders, selfless nurses, and compassionate physicians deeply committed to making healthcare better. Improving patient experience, employee engagement, and company culture are team sports; if we don't work together, this kind of work is impossible to accomplish. I use I Am The Patient Experience as a mindset, a mantra, something to remind me that change starts with me. It also inspires me to work with others to make a real difference. We can do so much more together than we ever could alone.

As I was reviewing and trying to organize over a hundred blog posts, I noticed a theme. No matter what the situation, job, or even interpersonal interaction, I try to leave it better than I found it. And so was born the title of the book. It's wonderful to feel I've made a difference in my little corner of the world, but if we team up, all work together for something bigger than ourselves, we can truly change the face of healthcare. I believe it's possible. Be the change.

Enjoy.

SECTION ONE:
THE CULTURE STORIES

I chose to divide this book into sections based on themes and The Culture Stories is my favorite section. To me, any discussion of improving patient experience has to begin with culture, so it's only natural that this is the opening section. Without a great culture, you're going to have a very hard time making any meaningful or lasting improvements in patient experience.

It makes me sad to even think it, but of all the places I've worked, (and there have been plenty), I think I've only found two or maybe three that had a really healthy culture. More often than not, the leader was a tyrant, the managers played favorites, or everything was reactive instead of proactive. Something was always keeping the organization from realizing its full potential.

It is horrible to work in a place with a bad culture. It doesn't take too long for good people to recognize it and get out, leaving behind the ones who are either actively creating it or are so entrenched in it, they can't see it. So it never changes.

As you'll read, I've worked in more than my fair share of healthcare organizations that didn't see the connection between how the actions of their leaders affected patient experience scores. All too often, they were looking for that 'quick fix' that would bump up the scores and make everyone feel like they were doing a great job.

Sadly, it just doesn't work that way.

Culture change can take anywhere from 3 to 7 years and most executives, at least the ones I've met, don't have an appetite for that. They want to see results now. One CEO for whom I worked actually wanted a daily printout of Patient Satisfaction scores. Daily. He wanted us to write policies, make changes, and adapt our strategy based on *daily* scores.

It was no surprise he and I butted heads.

Patient Experience doesn't exist in a vacuum. It's an indicator of your overall culture.

- Does your organization have a clear definition of patient experience? Does every staff member know it?

- In the hiring process, does attitude matter as much as skills and experience?

- How comfortable do staff feel speaking up when they feel something isn't right?

- How empowered are front-line staff in offering some service recovery when things don't go well?

- How visible and approachable are your executives?

- Does your organization treat its employees at least as well as it treats its patients?

- Is there a formal channel of feedback from the front line to the executives?

- Is there a robust and highly utilized system of reward and recognition for those who offer an exceptional experience?

Without these things in place, your organization will not have sustainable gains in its scores. You may see some wins, but you'll just as quickly see some losses, and every month will be a nail-biter, wondering how things will shake out.

A patient experience culture is the only way you'll know from one month to the next how your scores will go. *This is how we do things here* is the only mindset that will keep those scores consistently high, patients coming back, and employees feeling good about coming to work.

Quick fixes just won't cut it. Not in the long-term.

And the other big thing about culture I've learned: most of us think it has everything to do with the leadership team. They may outline what's expected, but it's those front-line folks that are the ones executing. Or not.

As far as the patient is concerned, that valet parker, that admissions clerk, that bedside nurse, that food service person, that housekeeper, and that case manager are your culture.

And it's not just that one nice nurse, that one helpful greeter, or that one kind radiology tech. It has to be *everyone*. Everywhere. Every encounter. Every time.

That's your culture. It starts with great leaders but it certainly doesn't end with them. It's also your people; how you select them, train them, grow and develop them, reward them, and counsel them.

As far as leadership, it's not just what you preach, it's what you tolerate.

As I tell my friends when they complain about their spouses: you get what you settle for.

I hope you enjoy this section of the book and it gives you some insight, and maybe even a chuckle.

DOING TO, DOING FOR, AND DOING WITH

I had the opportunity in 2017 to hear a speech from Jason Wolf, the head of the Beryl Institute, about where healthcare is going, specifically where Patient Experience efforts are headed. It was a wonderful talk and one of his slides in particular really resonated with me.

We in healthcare went from DO TO to DO FOR and now we're moving to DO WITH.

I really like that.

For a long time, medicine was all about fixing people who were sick. You went to see a doctor because something was wrong. Doctors were there to do things TO people.

Things started to change some years ago when we began to see medicine as more of a service. We started asking if patients were comfortable. We redesigned waiting areas and made all the inpatient rooms private. We utilized chaplains to address spiritual needs and social workers to assist with planning and care post-discharge. We even brought in animals for emotional support. Healthcare became something we can do FOR people.

Now we're in an age of patient engagement. We want patients to be in tune with their bodies and speak up if they feel something isn't right. Medicine is becoming more of a partnership. Instead of heading straight to the doctor's office, people are now looking up their symptoms online. They're asking more questions. They're seeking more second opinions. They're making more informed choices. Healthcare is something we're doing WITH people.

I really like that.

I know this can be difficult for physicians, especially if a patient's wishes fly in the face of his or her advice, or they've convinced themselves they have a certain disease because they read about it on the internet. It's hard to watch patients make decisions that aren't based in science.

So it's more important than ever to take the time to build trust, listen to what patients tell you is important to them, acknowledge how they feel, and give them accurate information to help them make good choices.

Instead of blindly following doctors' orders, patients are looking for support, advice, recommendations, and help; ultimately, the choice is theirs. When physicians and nurses start to see healthcare as something they do WITH people, instead of TO them or even FOR them, we will have achieved genuine patient engagement.

PATIENT-CENTEREDNESS

A few years ago while working at another health system, I got a phone call from an administrative assistant in one of our imaging offices. She asked about the courtesy van that the hospital provides to those who are in need of transportation but are unable to afford cab or bus fare. A patient who had been in before said she had no way to get home but had used that service and found it very helpful. This administrative assistant couldn't find the voucher she needed and was trying to hunt one down.

The hospital had recently changed its policy about which departments were authorized to give these vouchers out to patients. Apparently, people were taking advantage of them. Funny, I thought the whole idea of the vouchers was for people to take advantage of them... She called another department – one that was authorized – and asked if she could have a voucher for a patient who was here and needed to get home. The director responded with, "I don't know, I might get in trouble if I give this to you."

She had been in a meeting where the CFO was carrying on about how much money it costs every time someone uses this service and she got the message loud and clear that anyone caught giving the service to someone who didn't *really* need it would be in a whole lot of trouble. It was clear that managing the budget was more important than meeting a patient's needs.

I had to ask myself, what kind of a hospital is this? What do we truly value?

The administrative assistant called several more directors with no luck until someone decided that helping this patient get home was more important than potentially getting yelled at by an executive. Thankfully, this all happened behind the scenes; the patient had no idea there was such a scramble to find a simple voucher, but as I was listening to this story it became crystal clear to me that we had sent our employees the wrong message. All this talk about patient experience and putting the patient first... it's just talk.

Until employees – all employees – are empowered to take action that helps patients, you do not have a patient-centered organization and your patient experience efforts will go nowhere.

ANOTHER LOOK AT PATIENT-CENTEREDNESS

A while back, I wrote a piece about employees not wanting to do something kind for a patient for fear of getting in trouble. Recently, I saw, first-hand, employees not wanting to do something kind for a patient because they didn't think they had time for something that seemed so unimportant.

I was leaving the hospital at the end of the day when I happened upon a mom and her little boy who looking up at the ceiling. I did what anyone does when there are people looking up at the ceiling; I looked up at the ceiling. There, up out of reach, was a red balloon. The look on this boy's face was beyond sad. He didn't have to say a word. I knew I had to do something to help.

I walked a few feet around the corner to the information desk and asked the young woman if she would call maintenance and ask someone to get a ladder so we could get this little boy's balloon down for him. She looked at me for a moment before picking up the phone.

I could hear her side of the conversation. "Yeah, hi. Can you bring a ladder? (pause) It's for a balloon on the ceiling. (pause) Right. A balloon. (pause) I don't know, some kid. (longer pause) Oh. No?

Yeah, okay. Bye." She hung up the phone, looked at me and said, "They can't come, they're kinda busy. Sorry."

Frustrated, I walked back toward the boy and his mom, trying to come up with some other idea, when I saw a man from environmental services with a long push broom. He had seen the kid and, without even being asked, started to unscrew the head of his broom. He used the long handle to push the balloon down along the wall and into the boy's hands. You'd have thought he'd just given him a million dollars. We all thanked him profusely and he looked a little embarrassed, saying it was no big deal. But it meant the world to that family.

I couldn't stop thinking about this. I have no idea what brought this mom and her son to our hospital that day but even without knowing the specifics, we know that it's rarely good news that brings a mom and her young son to the hospital. And as much as I wanted to be angry at maintenance for not coming, they didn't see that boy's face, they didn't get a visual cue. Seeing him might have been enough to move them to action, but… really? Is that what it takes?

And the young woman at the information desk, I wanted to be upset with her, too. There was no sense of urgency in her voice, nothing that expressed the wonderful opportunity we had at that moment to make a lasting impression on this family. But she couldn't convey it because she didn't recognize it.

When we speak about patient experience, we talk primarily about physicians and nurses. Other staff, people who can make just as big an impact on patients and their families, are often an afterthought. Our examples in our training sessions are almost exclusively written for the clinical staff in an inpatient setting.

I wanted to be angry at our maintenance and reception staff but felt like I owned at least part of the blame for not making patient experience relatable to them. After all, they don't interact with patients the same way clinical staff does. They didn't commit to a career of saving lives and caring for people, right? I should have spent more time in our training classess and our new employee on-boarding talking about how impactful the non-clinical roles are.

And yet, a man who sweeps our hallway floors knew enough to take the head off his broom and push a balloon to a little kid. He didn't need patient experience training for that.

When we hire the right people, people who have a heart for service, patient experience training is almost redundant. It's not new information, but a reinforcement of what they already know. It's reminding them that they have hundreds of opportunities every single day to create a wonderful and lasting impression on people.

And even if there are people on staff who weren't born inherently knowing this, when the organizational culture is that of creating exceptional experiences for everyone, every time, people know to rise to the occasion and do a little something extra.

What disappointed me most about the balloon experience was that it was a very clear real-life example of how far we still had to go in our efforts.

OUR SCORES ARE BAD BECAUSE OF OUR PATIENTS

When you work in patient experience, you hear a lot of excuses for why scores are low:

- We were under construction and the noise was bad

- We had a lot of turnover and new staff wasn't properly trained

- We just merged with another big health system and there's a lot of uncertainty

- We're here to save our patients' asses, not kiss them

- Our hospital isn't as fancy as the one down the street, we need a makeover, we need private rooms, we need valet parking, we need…

- We were focused on getting ready for The Joint Commission visit

- Change takes time, we're getting there

As much as I've heard these used as valid reasons, they are things that we have some control over and can work to mitigate. Much of it has to do with communication, whether it's internal to the employees to set behavioral standards or external to the patients to help them understand what's happening and why.

So what really gets me is when we blame the patients for our inability to provide an acceptable experience for them:

- We have a really bad payor mix; they're all uninsured and homeless

- Our patients are all drug-seekers; they're mad we don't give them what they want

So it's *their* fault?

Hey, I know there are people out there who can be pretty unreasonable and difficult to please, but that doesn't mean we shouldn't try. I've seen far too many staff members immediately take an aggressive stance as soon as they realize their patient is uninsured, experiencing homelessness, or trying to manage chronic pain. They make assumptions and treat these patients a certain way and then wonder why they return an unfavorable survey.

And, incidentally, wealthier patients don't always make for happier ones. Years ago, I worked in a very fancy hospital in a very affluent area and found that those patients had much higher standards. They seemed far less tolerant when things didn't go as planned and much harder to please. But that doesn't mean we didn't try.

The bottom line is it doesn't matter what socioeconomic class of patient we're seeing. We should be doing our absolute best *every time* when it comes to serving our patients. And instead of blaming them for not having a good experience, we should be looking at ways we can better reach them. If we find our scores are low in a given demographic, it's on us to figure out how to improve.

Oh, there was one excuse in the top section that's actually true. Change takes time. You'll get there.

SILENCE ISN'T GOLDEN, IT'S PERMISSION

Much has been written about what leaders need to do in order to create lasting and meaningful change in an organization's culture. We know that leaders need to be clear about expectations, fully explain the 'why' behind the change, engage the hearts and minds of all employees, give frequent updates on progress, offer recognition along the way, etc. There's no shortage of instructions on what leaders need to do.

I'd like to talk about the things leaders sometimes don't do.

I've worked for many organizations that were trying to undergo a culture change. There were committees and cross-functional teams and retreats and kick-offs and balloons and all kinds of hoopla celebrating the new direction the company was taking. And there were plenty of dedicated people truly invested in seeing it happen. But many of them lacked something: the ability to speak up, call someone out, confront, correct. They were conflict-avoidant. And the changes they hoped for didn't stick.

It's hard to confront someone when he makes a comment that was acceptable yesterday but isn't today under the new culture change initiative. But you must. Everyone is watching. Everyone wants to know if this is for real or just another flash in the pan that fizzles out like the other programs that have come and gone.

When the executive leadership team stands up in front of everyone and talks about the new plan and how wonderful things are going to be but doesn't hold others – or themselves – accountable, they lose the confidence and trust of the whole team.

It isn't enough to compile a list of behavioral standards to follow. It has to be okay for people, regardless of their job title or position within the company, to – respectfully – call others out when they say or do something that isn't part of the new direction.

An old boss of mine had a framed saying on his wall right next to his desk. It said, "What you permit, you promote." If he saw something he knew didn't support the culture of the organization, he said something. He was always kind about it, but he didn't let it go. It's those little things, those daily interactions that shape culture and he knew it. He took a stand and made it okay for everyone else to do it, too.

If you're naturally conflict-avoidant (like I am), you might want to take a lesson from people you know who can gently, respectfully hold people accountable for their behavior. Notice their tone, the words they choose, the focus on the behavior not the person, and suggestions for how the situation might be handled differently. Notice how much they realize the importance of saying something.

Silence isn't golden, it's permission. What you permit, you promote.

GREAT LEADERS

Every so often, I'll see a post on LinkedIn that asks readers to name or describe the best leader they ever had. Thankfully, I've had several. But the one that really stands out for me is the president of a large medical center in suburban Chicago.

Although I only worked for him a short time, he left an indelible impression on me and is the one against whom all others are measured.

Why, I wonder? What was so great about him and his style?

It really all came down to just a few simple things.

1. He made it clear to me and to the other leaders that **my job mattered**. It was a new role and he consistently stressed how important it was to the hospital's success. I felt very connected to the higher purpose. Work was no longer work, it was a calling.

2. He got to know me and what motivated me. I felt like **he cared about me as a person**, not merely as someone who was there to do a job for him. I was much more willing to put in the extra effort because I didn't feel like a number.

3. He **held everyone accountable**. He held himself to some pretty high standards, especially when it came to staying professional and on top of things, and he expected the same from his leadership team. If you came to a meeting unprepared or said something unkind about another person, it simply wasn't tolerated. We were about results, integrity, support, and kindness.

4. He **didn't play favorites**. The rules didn't change depending on whether or not he liked you. No one got a free pass and no one was picked on.

5. He **inspired confidence**. He knew a lot about the industry and when he came up with a new idea, even something that seemed pretty 'out there', you didn't doubt that he could pull it off.

6. He **allowed you to make a mistake**. He created a safe space and if you happened to mess up, we talked about what exactly went wrong and how it could be avoided in the future. He never made you feel stupid, and encouraged you to keep trying something new.

I've since worked for some pretty great leaders, many of whom hit just about all of the things on this list. But he's really the one that stands out to me. I hope each of you reading this gets to work for someone just like this someday.

Better yet, you be that person. Don't just respond on LinkedIn with the name of a great leader; be one.

THE BEAUTY OF
MAKING MISTAKES

Something happened at the 2017 Grammy Awards show. I didn't see the whole thing, but I did see pop superstar Adele begin a tribute to the late George Michael, stop her performance, and start over. Having worked as a singer myself for a number of years, I couldn't imagine stopping in the middle of a song and asking the other musicians to please begin again. Lord knows I've wanted to.

This made me think about the tolerance we have for mistakes. In healthcare, it's practically zero. When there's a wrong-site surgery, an unexpected outcome, or even an unlikely but known risk factor, we do a root cause analysis, counsel those involved, suspend or even fire staff, and patients often sue.

I've worked in places where it wasn't safe to make a mistake. You got yelled at, embarrassed in front of your peers, pulled off a project, or fired. Did that make us more careful? Did we perform better? Nope.

We threw each other under the bus. We didn't contribute new ideas. We didn't speak up if we saw something that didn't look right. We worked long hours. We missed our kids' concerts and soccer games. We took our stress out on our spouses. We didn't sleep enough. We worked straight through lunch and came home too tired to eat dinner.

People will tell you they didn't learn nearly as much from their successes as they did from their mistakes. So why do so many companies rush to assign blame instead of looking at ways to make improvements?

Well for one, it's certainly easier to blame a person instead of a process. Holding the system accountable means that changes need to be made, often expensive ones, and many people don't want to admit the system is broken when they're the ones who designed it.

Certainly, if there is a willful, deliberate action taken that causes harm, people need to be held accountable. But so often, mistakes are just that – mistakes. It makes sense to look at the bigger picture and see what could have been done differently both from an individual and systems perspective.

But it has to be safe, not punitive.

Adele felt safe enough in her star-power to stop an entire orchestra on live TV and ask them to start again. Whether the problem was in not getting her starting pitch because of a bad earpiece or simply due to nerves, she demonstrated that it's better to speak up, go back and do the job right, even if it means suffering a little embarrassment. The public doesn't seem to be holding it against her.

Let's hope more organizations take the same approach.

WHEN THE CEO IS A JERK

I've been fortunate to have worked for some really great bosses in my life; people who were truly invested in developing their people and consistently put the needs of the organization above their own. Capable, charismatic, servant leaders who praised in public and corrected in private and always managed to get everyone excited about the mission. Not coincidentally, those were the most successful organizations.

And then there were those bosses who were just plain terrible. Theory X tyrants who were all stick and no carrot. No one felt safe to disagree or even speak up at a meeting unless it was to say "Yes, sir!" Directors were routinely demeaned and embarrassed in front of their peers; they then did the same to the managers who, in turn, would do it to the front line staff.

It was miserable.

I wish I could tell you that I always carried myself with quiet dignity and grace. I didn't. But now that I'm a little older and wiser, I've been able to come up with some ways to stay sane when working in a less than ideal environment.

1. Remember to **stay professional**. Even if the boss is name-calling, swearing a blue streak, or belittling people who aren't in the room, he's still the boss and lowering yourself to his level isn't going to serve you well. It's easy to let yourself get swallowed up into this kind of culture, thinking that's what it takes to succeed. Don't do it. A boss like this might appear to like you for acting like him, but he can just as easily turn on you and make you his next target. And by then, you've alienated your coworkers.

2. Remind yourself that **her opinion of you isn't really you**. Most people go into work wanting to do a good job, be successful and impress the boss. So when the boss has nothing encouraging or positive to say about you, it can be hard to remember that you are capable, talented and better than this. Remember: her words are a reflection of her, not you.

3. **Don't give up.** Instead of letting the negativity sap you of your motivation (which is *really* easy to let happen), stay focused on doing the great work you were hired to do. You may not receive the recognition you want, but continue to take pride in your work. Spend your energy on your projects, not on playing the victim and complaining about how awful it is.

4. **Focus on your behavior, not his.** If you make it your personal mission to change the culture of the organization by trying to change the boss, I'm afraid you're in for a rude awakening. In my experience, people who speak up in that environment are escorted out. Instead, model the behavior you wish to see. People learn more from your example than from your words.

5. Most importantly, make plans to **get out**. When the person at the top fosters a culture this toxic and counter-productive, it can take a real toll on your health. Insomnia, upset stomach, overeating, high blood pressure, stress – no job is worth it. You owe it to yourself to move on and find a company that takes care of its employees.

A bad boss makes for a tough situation but stay strong, stay positive and stay focused on the future.

KEEP ON KEEPIN' ON

The work of culture change, whether it's within a hospital or any other organization, is tough. It starts out with a lot of excitement and energy; there are meetings about mission statements, brainstorming exercises on behaviors, and several power point iterations of the training program before unveiling the final product. The training sessions are the easy part. We design them to be fun, participatory, and a repositioning of what most of us learned as children: be nice to your coworkers, treat customers well, and don't let your mood dictate your manners.

Sustainability, well, that's the hard part.

No matter how much you involve front-line staff in the development of the program, there will always be people who resist. Plenty of books have been written about the importance of leaders holding their teams accountable to the new behavioral standards. We've been taught how to have those conversations with low performers and help them either move up or move on. We know about using behavioral-based interviewing to hire the right people. We have no shortage of books to help leaders lead.

What if the issue isn't front-line staff?

Your organization is full of directors and vice presidents who moved into those positions under the 'old' way of doing things, before your culture change program came to town. And they're very invested in remaining in those positions. So, while they'll give your program lip-service and convince the president they're on board, they may be the ones who are really struggling with this new way of doing things.

They may feel very threatened by all the change but they know they have to get behind it if they want to stay in those roles. So rather than attack the program, they may attack you. I hear it all the time from my friends who do this kind of consulting work. When things get too unsettling for middle management, the conversation shifts and the focus moves from the product to the person. It becomes more about how unlikeable that consultant is and less about the content of the material.

Be patient with these people. They have a lot invested in their jobs and they're used to doing things a certain way. Plus, the pressure is on them when it comes to holding their teams accountable. They're under a microscope, much more than the front line, when it comes to sustaining change. They're nervous. They're threatened. They're human.

Don't take it personally. Their attacks aren't as much about you as they are about them. You keep doing the work you know you were meant to do. Keep trying to make the world a better place, one organization at a time. Some people aren't ready to make the change. But don't let them slow you down.

HOW LEADING REMOTELY IS REDEFINING COMPANY CULTURE

As of this writing, most of us are sheltering in place and working from home due to COVID-19. Non-clinical hospital leaders, including the patient experience professionals, may be coming to the hospital a couple of days a week, but we're doing most of our work from our living rooms over Zoom. So without being there, how do we know things are getting done?

Early in my career, I worked under several bosses who felt they needed to micromanage everything my colleagues and I did. Every moment between 8:30am and 5:00pm had to be accounted for or the assumption was we were slacking off. I always had a pretty good work ethic and wasn't motivated to work out of fear. I did the job because I enjoyed the job and wanted to keep learning. I realize not everyone thinks that way.

But those colleagues of mine who didn't have that same attitude didn't do great work under that kind of micromanaging. They found ways to game the system and make it look like they were working. And they mostly got away with it. At some point, they might have gotten found out but that only brought the hammer down harder. I had to ask myself why they didn't just let them go? Why spend your whole day surveilling your staff when you could be doing more important things?

When I came into leadership, one of the best things I did was hire people who appeared to have a work ethic like mine. People who got the job done without having to be watched like a hawk. People who had a passion for the work and who wanted to keep getting better at it. People I knew I didn't need to micromanage.

And guess what – work got done. I had a great team who understood the expectations, had the tools they needed, knew they could come to me with questions, and were recognized and celebrated for doing a good job. I could spend my time setting the strategic direction of the department instead of yelling at them for coming in ten minutes late.

And now that I'm not physically in the hospital, watching to be sure leader rounds are happening and staff are using AIDET in every interaction, I have to trust that they're doing it because they know it's the right thing to do, not because they'll get in trouble if they don't.

For those managers who came up through the ranks thinking that they always had to be looking over their employees' shoulders, always there monitoring their every move lest they start goofing off, this new normal should be proof positive that that style of leadership doesn't work. It never has. Anyone can get compliance, what matters is commitment.

I don't know what work will look like when this is over, but working remotely has forced micromanagers to trust their employees and change their style of leadership. It's about time. I'm sorry it took a pandemic to do it.

DO YOU NEED A DIRECTOR?

If your hospital is part of a larger health system with many hospitals in several states, should there be a Director of Patient Experience in each of them? Do you need a director-level position if the overall vision and program strategy is done at a regional or national level, or could you do just fine with a coordinator or a specialist managing the day-to-day drivers of improvement? If you have a dedicated person inside the walls of each hospital, does patient experience become that person's job instead of everyone's?

When I held the director-level position, it was primarily at independent hospitals, those not tied to a larger health system. I, along with the local executive team, set the strategy, created the training tools, selected the vendors for our electronic rounding programs, and structured the accountability standards. In a larger system, all of those things are done at the national or regional level, with very little room for variability at the local level.

When all of those decisions are being made at a higher level, why have a director at each hospital? You could make the argument that a director who sits on the operational leadership team has more influence and will be able to more effectively lead culture change within the walls of the hospital than a specialist-level would. You could say that it sends a message to staff that patient experience is important and that's why there's a director in charge of it.

But when there's a high level person in that role, it often becomes solely his or her responsibility. Staff tend to say, "This is a patient experience issue. It's not my job, call her," when the reality is, of course, it's everyone's job.

If it were a coordinator or a specialist, you can more easily make the argument that the directors over each unit and department have to take ownership of patient experience results. The specialist can offer support and assistance by providing data, offering training, and assisting in service recovery, but the directors have the ultimate responsibility of ensuring that staff deliver on the promise of an exceptional experience.

And specialists aren't in charge of setting the strategic direction. They get the tools from the national or regional level and are charged with executing on those tools. It can be difficult for a director to act on a prepackaged toolkit about which they had no input, especially if they've had that responsibility previously.

If the goal of the large multi-site health system is consistency across the enterprise, it will do just fine to set the strategy, create the training, design the toolkit, and analyze the data at the system level. Create director positions at the regional level to serve as consultants for lower performing hospitals and then have a specialist or coordinator at each hospital to keep things running smoothly.

How does your hospital manage its patient experience efforts?

THEY ALREADY KNOW

There's a conversation happening in healthcare about transparency. It isn't new. The conversation has been going on for years, but we all still can't agree about how to handle negative patient comments and reviews or even whether patients should be part of our committees.

In every Patient and Family Advisory Council I've ever run, I've met some resistance when it comes to bringing members of the community onto our quality committees, specifically the Patient Safety and the Grievance committees. The heads of those groups tend to be particularly skittish about letting people outside of the hospital hear about all the things that didn't go quite right during an inpatient hospital stay.

Same thing with publishing negative patient comments or addressing online negative reviews. I used to work for an organization that would remove every negative review that appeared online. They didn't respond to them; they simply removed them. They scoured Facebook, Yelp, and all the other sites and if a less-than-perfect review popped up, they had it deleted. There was no statement like, "We're sorry your experience wasn't up to par; please contact our patient advocate so we can better address your concerns." Nope. It was just deleted.

Other organizations have struggled with publishing the negative comments that appear on patient surveys. They were happy to print the good ones, but wouldn't go near the bad ones. And all the while, in all these different places, I kept asking, "Do they really think patients don't know this stuff?"

The conversation about your hospital is happening, whether you're listening or not.

They've stayed overnight with us. They've been in our ER. They saw that physician. They know exactly what's going on here. We shouldn't be afraid to let them sit in while we air our dirty patient safety laundry. Whether we post the bad reviews or not, they know what's happening.

People in the checkout line at the grocery store are talking about your hospital. Parents of kids in the same class at school are comparing notes. Men and women are making recommendations or offering a warning to their friends about the doctors on your staff. By letting them sit in on your internal committees, you're letting them get a little more information about the inner-workings of your hospital, instead of relying solely on what people are saying.

Make them part of the solution. If you think you're shielding them from the negative stuff, you're wrong. Trust me, they already know.

TREATING PATIENT EXPERIENCE LIKE A RISK EVENT

One of the great things about having a long career in a single industry is being able to see all the changes and improvements that were made over the years. I've been in non-clinical healthcare roles for more than 20 years, always with a focus on patients and their families.

Early on, it was all about quality and safety. We wanted better than expected outcomes and zero harm for our patients, which are wonderful goals, don't get me wrong. But there was very little, if any, thought given to patient experience or employee engagement. We used to think that patients would be happy simply because we performed a successful surgery or cured whatever illness they had. *"Hey, you didn't die. Be happy we saved your life."* And we weren't all that interested in how the staff was doing either. *"Hey, this is just part of the job. Be happy you have a job."* A former boss actually said that to me once after a particularly difficult case. Seriously.

These days, it's so inspiring and affirming to see the industry putting these four domains: safety, quality, patient experience, and staff engagement, on the same plane. There is undeniable evidence and, according to the 2018 Strategic Blueprint for Transformational Change from Press Ganey, "...performance in each domain does not take place in a silo, but rather, drives and is driven by performance in the others."

Just about every hospital I know has a daily safety huddle, where people in all departments come together for a few minutes every day to discuss safety issues and potential risks. More and more, they're adding patient experience to the mix and identifying areas where they need to implement service recovery or proactively get out and address an issue before it becomes a bigger problem.

And at national healthcare conferences, I see more and more breakout and keynote sessions about addressing employee engagement and preventing staff burnout. It's wonderful to see these changes and I'm so encouraged to see how far we've come over the years.

Safety, quality, patient experience and staff engagement. When the goals of all four are aligned, integrated, and given equal weight, all kinds of wonderful things begin to happen: patients start to experience what they want and expect from us and we are reconnected to our purpose of having chosen to work in healthcare. It's an exciting time, one I'm glad to be able to experience.

DO SERVICE FAILURES REALLY MATTER?

One of the unfortunate realities of working in healthcare is that bad things happen. There are wrong-site surgeries, medication errors, and unexpected deaths, to name a few. Thankfully, they don't happen often; we work hard to keep people safe, so when things like this happen, we do a lot of investigation.

Often, these things aren't one person's fault; they're a combination of processes that failed or actions not taken, so we do something we call an RCA, or root cause analysis. It's designed to not place the blame on an individual, but to look at processes and where we can improve.

We create a timeline of events, gather the people who were involved, outline the contributing factors, and discuss what we knew and when we knew it. It's easy to fall into hindsight, but we have to keep in mind that certain details weren't known at the time. We also come up with ideas for preventing this from happening again.

RCAs are good things. They result in change, improvement, learning, and the chance for the staff to come to terms with what is often an emotional situation.

It occured to me recently that we don't have the same kind of analysis after a service failure.

When it comes to patient complaints and grievances, we apologize, maybe take some money off the bill, talk to the person against whom the complaint was made, do a little coaching, and that's about it. We don't do nearly the amount of problem-solving that we do with quality and safety events.

Why is that?

For starters, I think we still believe that good service is a nice-to-have, not a have-to-have in healthcare. There are still plenty of clinicians who feel that if you didn't die, you've got no reason to complain.

I think the bigger issue, though, is that it's just harder to measure. It's easy to know when something that is never supposed to happen happens. Quality issues are easy to measure; did you end the surgery with the same number of sponges you started with? Was the right dose of medication delivered at the right time and by the right route? These are yes-no questions.

Service isn't so simple. They've tried to make it black and white with checklists that contain all the steps in AIDET and all the evidence-based practices we strive to do. Did you knock before entering the patient's room? Check. Did you round on the patient every hour? Check. Did you manage-up the previous nurse who's going home for the day? Check.

All of these are good, but they don't guarantee the patient will have a good experience. Sometimes we do these things but in a manner that comes off as insincere. It happened, but the patient didn't feel it. How do you measure that?

Patient experience is a gray area in an industry that prefers black and white. When she complains, we say,"She was just crabby. We did everything we could do and we still couldn't make her happy. That's just how some people are." And that's that. We shrug our shoulders and say, "Oh well," and put her in the They'll-Never-Be-Satisfied bucket. No real investigation, no problem solving, no improvement plan.

We just don't see service events as being as serious as quality ones. And until we do, we will continue to have them.

Can you imagine how things would change if we did an RCA on every patient complaint? It feels impossible and overwhelming now but, if we did them consistently, we'd have fewer and fewer of them.

Does your health system treat them differently?

THE RCA GONE WRONG

I've written before about Root Cause Analysis, those things hospitals do when there's a serious safety event. A good RCA will include a description of the event, a timeline of everything that happened leading up to the event, all of the people involved, an investigative team, a report out that focuses on process, not people, and asks 'why' until you get to the root of the issue, and plans for corrective action.

They're good things to do. When done well, the participants leave with a better understanding of where the process broke down and what steps they can take to improve that process. Staff who had been struggling with guilt or regret often feel much better afterwards because they had a chance to see how other factors contributed to the event. Silos are broken down as a result of people from many departments coming together and examining how their individual efforts affected the outcome.

Staff feel supported by leadership and empowered to make changes when RCAs are done well.

But what if they're not?

I participated in an RCA a few years ago that ended up doing more harm than good because of a poor facilitator.

It was a terribly sad case; a patient came in with a seemingly minor issue requiring some routine surgery but suffered an arrest in the operating room and didn't survive. In the days that followed, there was a lot of finger pointing. Rumors were swirling around throughout the hospital. The staff who were involved were feeling terrible about the outcome and unsupported by their leader. It was a very messy situation.

The Vice President of Patient Safety and Risk scheduled the RCA as he always did and included everyone who had been involved but this time, something was different; the president wanted to attend. He hadn't had any involvement in the case but wanted to see and hear what was discussed at the RCA. If this had been a president who was visible, approachable, and routinely involved in the day-to-day activities at the hospital, this wouldn't have been uncomfortable. But this president was none of those things. Having him there inhibited the participants and made them feel even more like they were under attack.

When we started talking about how things broke down and began to ask those "why" questions, the president chimed in and asked, "Why, if that was your responsibility, did you not do it?" The VP tried to jump in and bring the focus back to the process, not the person, but the president wouldn't let it go. It was easy to scapegoat this particular nurse, but if you took a step back, you could see there was a bigger issue here. Many things were going on at that moment and we, as the investigators, have to see it from the perspective of what was happening as it was happening now, not from the benefit of hindsight.

The RCA continued in much the same way, with the president asking very pointed questions to the people in the room about their personal responsibility for the outcome instead of looking at the many different ways the process failed. As much as the VP tried to keep things on track, he simply couldn't get control of the meeting. It was a disaster. We left the room feeling worse than we did when we entered with no real resolution or plan for corrective action.

I can't speak for the president but I suspect he left feeling very satisfied that he got to what he thought was the issue: a bad nurse. I can't begin to describe what a huge step backwards this RCA was, not only for staff morale but for patient safety. When staff feels that they will be blamed for every mistake and there is no tolerance for error, they don't perform better, they perform far worse.

A culture of safety is so much more than zero harm. It's staff who are empowered to speak up when they see something wrong. It's channels that make it easy to report an issue or a near-miss, along with a feedback loop so employees know that action is being taken. It's processes in place with several steps along the way to catch mistakes before they reach a patient. It's leaders who don't set out to find a scapegoat when things do go wrong. It's providing safe spaces for staff to talk through events once they've occurred. It's staff working across their departments, together, to keep patients safe. It's everyone working together, focused on patient safety throughout the continuum of care.

I've participated in many more RCAs since this one and am happy to say they go well much more often than they go wrong. But when they go wrong, it takes a very long time to recover.

AM I AN ESSENTIAL WORKER?

Like many people, I've been looking at the job market since COVID-19 struck. I look at the types of jobs being posted, I talk to people interviewing for patient experience roles, and I've seen in my own community the kinds of positions being filled. In a pandemic, who is an essential worker?

Being in healthcare, I've taken a great interest in which hospital positions are prioritized and which are put on the back-burner until we get our arms around COVID. Sadly, it came as no surprise to me that patient experience postings were put on hold or completely eliminated. I fear we still have a lot of work to do when it comes to demonstrating our value.

But what really struck me was how the tourist and hospitality industries are hiring like mad for servers, front desk staff, housekeepers, and even concierge roles. I'm not knocking the concierge, but in the age of the internet, I'm very capable of making my own dinner reservation, thank you. Is a concierge more essential than a patient experience director?

I currently live in a tourist town and the local luxury hotel has been on a hiring spree ever since they re-opened in mid-May, after closing for six weeks due to COVID. We had no idea at the time how much longer we'd be sheltering in place, and people were starting to think maybe it was okay to start going out again, have dinner at a restaurant, maybe even take a quick vacation. From what I understand from the staff, ever since June, every day has been like the 4th of July. That resort has been at full capacity every night. They can't hire people fast enough to keep up with the incredible demand.

At the same time, I was talking with my healthcare colleagues about their staffing and learning that many, many positions were facing reduction in hours, furlough, and even becoming completely eliminated. A few friends who were interviewing for patient experience leadership roles were learning those positions were being placed on hold indefinitely.

So in order for a luxury hotel to operate effectively, they need to hire a team of concierges, but a large healthcare system feels it can do alright without anyone leading the patient experience effort? Am I an essential worker?

Certainly, I understand the difference between the two. One is a luxury, paid for directly by the consumer. The other is a complex myriad of third-party payers with a lot of charitable care in the mix, not to mention a reduction in more profitable elective surgeries. I get it. But what I'm left with is the feeling that we in the patient experience sector still haven't yet convinced the establishment how valuable we are.

In addition to just being the right thing to do, when done right, patient experience improves the bottom line in a number of ways.

1. Higher H-CAHPS scores mean better reimbursement. Like it or not, better scores mean more medicare dollars. There's 25% of 2% being withheld from CMS that hospitals can

earn back through their patient experience results. 25% of 2% doesn't sound like a lot, but trust me, it is.

2. Better patient experience starts with better employee engagement. Hospitals with engaged employees experience less turnover. Recruiting, hiring, training, and on-boarding is expensive.

3. Better patient experience means fewer patient safety incidents. Engaged, caring staff make fewer medication errors, and have more proactive measures in place to prevent events like pressure ulcers and unattended falls.

4. Better patient experience means fewer lawsuits. Patients are far less likely to sue if they like their care team, feel they've been treated respectfully, and were communicated with in a compassionate, transparent manner.

5. Great patient experience means higher Yelp and other social media reviews, which creates an increase in new patients. An increase in market share not only increases revenue but helps a hospital's purchasing power, as well.

6. Great patient experience creates loyalty and repeat business. Patients are far less likely to change providers or hospitals when they've had a good experience previously.

I'm sure there are plenty more I've forgotten – more evidence that we have work to do when it comes to stating our case. This isn't just window dressing. We are no longer a nice-to-have, we are a have-to-have. We are essential employees. At least as essential as the concierge.

TRASH ON THE FLOOR

Some years ago when I first started working in patient experience, I was with an organization that wanted to, among other things, change its culture. The Director of Human Resources was concerned about the low employee engagement scores and high turnover. She approached the CEO about making some changes designed to improve our patient satisfaction scores and make staff enjoy coming to work.

As the newly-minted Manager of Patient Experience, I was brought in on the team to help lead the change. I had just come from a healthcare system that had engaged the Studer Group and I saw some great successes there with the Studer model.

While we were all sitting around the big conference room table trying to come up with ideas, I brought up one of the things that stuck with me and still does to this day: if you see a piece of trash on the floor, pick it up. It may seem like a small thing but it speaks to the overall sense of ownership and pride an employee feels by working there. It's not 'someone else's job'. I work here. It's my job. When I see things that are wrong, I take action and make them right.

My suggestion was met with deafening silence. The COO finally spoke up and said, "If this doesn't directly make patient experience scores go up, I don't want to invest one minute of energy into it."

It was then I knew we had a problem.

Sometimes, when you're trying to change a culture, you do things that appear to be insignificant or even silly, but they're things that build on a feeling. When you pick trash up off the floor, you're not only reinforcing the idea of accountability, you're demonstrating that no job is 'beneath' you. It's not someone else's job to pick up trash, it's not someone else's job to answer that call light, and it's not someone else's job to handle this angry patient. If you see something, you do something.

When employees are empowered to step outside their job description and fix something that needs fixing, it strengthens their sense of pride, commitment, and feeling of belonging within an organization. To this day, I can't walk down the halls of a hospital and not pick up trash when I see it. And when others see me model that behavior, they do it, too.

What seemingly insignificant behaviors are you encouraging your employees to do? They matter. Believe me.

TACTICS VS. CULTURE

I had a conversation with a senior leader not long ago; we were talking about what kind of an organization we wanted to be, what kind of talent we wanted to draw, what we wanted patients to think of us. I mentioned that I'd worked for a hospital with many clearly defined expectations and standards that at first seemed uncomfortable but eventually became habits.

Certain things were so ingrained at that hospital that they became a natural part of me even in other places. I've mentioned this before, but if we saw any kind of trash on the floor – paper, wrappers, anything – we were expected to pick it up instead of walk past it in the hope that someone from environmental services would come around soon. I haven't worked for them for several years but I still pick up trash when I see it on the floor.

It was a concrete illustration of how culture is formed.

When we think of patient experience merely as a series of tactics designed to raise scores, we've not only missed the point, we've put the cart in front of the horse. We were trying to shape our organization's future, define what we want to become. That can't be expressed merely in a series of things you can measure, it's more than that.

It starts by having employees take pride in where they work. Part of that means acting like an owner and taking action when you see something wrong, like trash on the floor. It may seem like a small thing but it's those small things that add up to create your organization's culture. When you step outside of your expressed job responsibilities and take action when something is wrong, you're more engaged, you're part of something larger than yourself. That's a big part in creating a positive, patient-centered culture with employees who feel connected to purpose.

The employees at that organization still walk past trash on the floor. Patient experience scores still haven't improved. Think there's a connection?

MOVING THE NEEDLE

How do you create lasting change in an organization? What's the 'secret sauce' when it comes to delivering on quality, safety, and patient experience?

By now, you know that I've worked in a lot of different hospitals and health systems. I've been fortunate to have worked for some really high performing organizations that were firing on all cylinders, and I've worked for some incredibly dysfunctional places that just couldn't get out of their own way.

I've seen the same tactics rolled out over and over again: hourly rounding, bedside shift report, sit a bit, it takes two rounding, AIDET, multidisciplinary rounds, updated whiteboard, and on and on. For those of you who aren't familiar with these terms, it doesn't really matter. These were things that were dreamed up with the very best of intentions, designed to improve the patient experience. And, when done correctly, really do have a positive impact.

Here's the thing.

Not one of these things is going to work without relationship. Not relationship between nurses and patients, relationship between nurses and leadership.

When tactics like these are rolled out as edicts, without leadership soliciting any input from staff or developing any kind of dialogue about why these things are important, they become check-the-box exercises. They're done because they have to be done, but there's no real connection or meaning behind it. That defeats the whole purpose.

If I am brand new to an organization and I walk up and introduce myself to a unit manager by saying, "Hi, I'm the new patient experience director and I'm here to make sure you and your staff are doing hourly rounds. Can I see your rounding logs, please?", do you think I'm going to make a new friend? Is this nurse manager going to see me as a person who is there to support her or a person who is there to monitor her?

I'm not the rounding police. I don't care if she and her staff have checked the box and rounded on every patient. I care that she and her staff have connected in a meaningful way with those patients, but I won't be able to support her in those efforts if we are not in the right relationship. It's up to me to help her connect the dots between hourly rounding and delivering an exceptional experience. She needs to know that she can count on me to help remove the barriers that may be keeping her staff from spending quality time with patients.

How do I do it? Be visible, accessible, approachable, open, curious. Develop and maintain a relationship. Listen. Be open about what I can and cannot do. Deliver on what I promise. That's it. That's the secret sauce.

Somewhere along the road, front line staff came to distrust leadership. As leaders, it's up to us to build that trust back up. When staff know that we care about them and what they're dealing with, they are far more likely to do the things we're asking of them. Sure, we could take a 'crack the whip' approach and demand that they do these things or be fired, but that's not what's going to move the needle on patient experience. Not over the long-term, anyway. You'll get compliance but you won't get commitment.

The patient experience is a reflection of your culture. Don't focus on the scores, focus on the problem.

NO WORDS

A lot is happening in the world right now. I've spent the last few blogs writing about COVID-19 and, while many cities are opening back up, new cases are still being diagnosed every day. And in the midst of all the division and politicizing about mask-wearing and whether or not certain businesses can reopen, we've had at least three high-pro-file cases of police brutality and blatant, unrepentant racism.

This is far from the first time an innocent man of color was murdered while in police custody or chased down by white vigilan-tes and killed in the middle of the street. Our country has a long and ugly history of these very things. But more and more people are speaking up and demanding change. It's important.

It's important that all people, not just African-Americans, speak up, join the fight, donate money, support the cause. But it's even more important that we start doing a better job of listening.

I'm no expert on race matters. I can't pretend to know what it feels like to be black in America. So if I am to understand and be more effective in trying to change the system, it's time to do more listening. There are thousands of voices out there, screaming to be heard. They don't need our opinion, they need our support, and we can best support by listening. Listen for truth, listen to understand, listen with humility.

These are the same skills I use when I work with patient complaints. I wouldn't dream of arguing with a patient who tells me they had a bad experience with us. I would never say, "Well yeah you had a bad time, but so did that patient over there; be glad that wasn't you." I would never tell them they were blowing it out of proportion or that it doesn't happen all that often or it's a lot better than it used to be.

I would never tell them that the system works just fine and then not do anything to remedy their complaint. And I would never blame the people who bring us the concerns and think it was their problem, not ours.

It's difficult to hear negative things about the place you work or the people you work with or even about yourself. The first reaction is typically to get defensive and gather up as much evidence as you can to prove the opposite. But that doesn't bring you any closer to solving the problem.

When a person who has difficulty walking tells me that navigating the hallways of our hospital is nearly impossible, I don't brush it off thinking, "Hey most people can walk just fine and don't have any problems," and then do nothing.

When we want to get a better handle on what it's like to be a parent of a newborn in the ICU, we don't all sit around the table and try to imagine it, ourselves. We contact people who have lived that experience and when we ask them what we can do better, we listen to them. Sometimes, their solutions are easy. But most of the time, they're tough, time-consuming, and expensive.

But we do them because we know it's the right thing to do. We take responsibility for having caused the issue in the first place and we work to fix it.

Novelist and activist James Baldwin said, "Not everything that is faced can be changed, but nothing can be changed until it is faced." Such an obvious concept when it comes to customer service, patient experience, or process improvement, but so difficult when it comes to race relations and systemic oppression.

Certainly, rules and laws are needed but they alone won't solve the problem. We need to face the fact that we have a problem. We need to change people's hearts. It begins with listening.

SECTION TWO:
THE TACTICS STORIES

It's no surprise to me that this is my largest section. I am no stranger to tactics. It takes tactics to make changes, but, as I said in the last section, none of those tactics will last without a supportive culture.

We're all looking for that magic bullet, that thing that will miraculously make the scores go through the roof.

It's just not that easy.

This is hard work. It takes time. And it takes a commitment from every member of the executive leadership team to make it happen.

When I go to patient experience conferences, more often than not, the breakout sessions are all about tactics. "Here's what we did at our hospital and our scores went from X to Y in just 3 months."

Useful, yes. But just as you can't put a roof on a house without a foundation first, you can't implement meaningful, sustainable tactics without a good culture. We've become so focused on the scores, we've forgotten why we measure them in the first place.

An old boss of mine said as we were developing the training for the staff, "Sometimes you have to cut the meat small." It surprises me how often I use that phrase when we're talking about tactics. There are people who just naturally get this stuff and go out of their way to provide an exceptional experience, but there are others who may have the right intentions but who struggle with exactly how to convey them.

It turns out, you *can* teach this stuff. Anyone willing to learn can learn. For them, it's not enough to tell them to be nice. Everyone thinks they're nice. But telling them to introduce themselves when they enter a patient room and call the patient by name, that's cutting the meat small. That's something practical they can do and most of them will.

So I don't mean to jam on the tactics. They're useful. They're helpful. But they, themselves, are not going to get the job done. They're only the platform to connection. It takes connection to deliver an exceptional patient experience. Let's measure the outcomes, not the tactics that get us there.

Enjoy The Tactics Stories.

MANAGEMENT BY CHECKLIST

In the world of patient experience, we have a lot of evidence-based best practices that we're constantly measuring: bedside shift report, hourly nurse rounding, MD-RN team rounds, leader rounding, and more. We spend a lot of time checking off boxes on the checklist to be sure all of those things are being done.

It's important that we do these things. But how do we get people not only to do these things but do them well?

I've seen far too many managers send out communications that outline a process and direct people to action but few that have been all that compelling. That may be management but it's not leadership.

The thing that moves people to action isn't always a directive. And even if they do start moving, there's no guarantee they'll be moving effectively.

We make lasting change through relationships. People are far more likely to make a change when they understand the reason behind it and trust the person leading the change.

When we spend time with staff, understand what drives them, recognize the challenges they face, and get to know them as people, we begin to earn their trust. I'm far more likely to get behind a leader who knows me than one I've never even seen.

The checklists aren't enough. Help your team connect to the why. When leaders lead with trust, mutual respect and connection, they create teams who not only make the change but do it well, with intention and purpose.

MORE ABOUT THE CHECKLIST

Last time, I wrote about management by checklist. I stressed the importance of relationships and helping your team connect to the 'why' behind the directives.

This time I'd like to expand on that and talk about the number of things that are on that checklist.

A few years ago, I was working at a hospital that really wanted to improve their patient experience scores (their words, not mine) so they decided to make a list of all the things that have been shown to do so: AIDET, hourly nurse rounding, bedside shift report, MD-RN rounds, leader rounds, empathy statements, in-the-moment coaching, physician shadowing... the list went on and on. At the end of the exercise, I think there were 28 things they wanted to implement.

I asked them what they wanted to start with. "We're doing them all!"

"All?" I asked. "We're starting with all of them?"

"Yep, we're going to shake things up all across the board," they answered. "We've designed checklists to ensure that everyone is doing these things and we're going to see an amazing jump in our scores, just you watch."

The next week our nurse leaders were presented with a list of 28 things they needed to start doing and monitoring. Some of those things were already in place but happening inconsistently, others were new. We didn't leave a lot of time for training; most of the instructions were given verbally at the time of the rollout.

There was a blitz, with many units trying hard to do everything on the list, but after just a few weeks, they ran out of steam. Too many plates spinning, too many things falling off, and too many opportunities to fail.

Had we just gone with one or two at a time, given them time to become a habit, and let them see some success before adding another, I think we would have had a very different outcome.

When we give our teams too many things to accomplish, they end up accomplishing nothing.

SEE THE BIGGER PICTURE

It's funny, when you've been working in the same field for a number of years, it's easy to get a little lost in the weeds.

So much of the work of patient experience can get swallowed up in tactics: hourly rounding, daily huddle, communication training, physician shadowing, etc. There is so much to do every day, whether it's resolving a formal grievance within seven days, responding to the comments patients have submitted on our surveys, or compiling the next batch of data to present to the executive team, we can get caught up in the day-to-day and forget about the bigger and more meaningful picture.

Don't get me wrong; all of these tactics are good things, but they can distract us from what it really takes to deliver an exceptional patient experience: people.

I've watched staff go through the AIDET checklist, reciting everything on the script without a hint of sincerity. I've seen nurses poke their heads in patient rooms and ask, "Everything alright?" and before the patient has a chance to answer, they're halfway down the hallway, checking off the boxes on their hourly rounding sheet.

I've proofread some letters physicians have written in response to a patient grievance that didn't have a note of compassion.

The point is, none of these tactics matter if the wrong people are delivering them. People, the right people, have to be the non-negotiable when we're trying to move the needle on improvement. The words we use when we post a position, the questions we ask during an interview, the on-boarding process, effective and inspiring leaders at every level, and our continued recognition and re-engagement of our teams, help us ensure we have the right people carrying out the message that patients are the reason we're here. How they feel is important to us.

The overarching strategy of any healthcare organization has to be keeping its employees connected to purpose. We have to remind them every day that these are people who need our help, our compassion, our patience. They're vulnerable, frightened, in pain, overwhelmed. We are there to serve them.

Tactics can help focus our efforts, but when we allow the tactics to become merely simple check-the-box exercises without any personal connection behind them, we've lost. We've gotten swallowed up in the weeds.

Don't lose sight of the big picture. Remember why you're there and help others remember, too.

WHAT ARE WE CELEBRATING?

Not long ago, I was at a patient experience conference and decided to sit in on a breakout session given by a hospital that had recently received an award for raising their H-CAHPS scores. We're all looking for the secret sauce and I was interested in hearing how they did it.

The two presenters talked about how they took a specific question from the survey and made that their focus. They conducted huddles on that question at the start and end of every shift, they measured and posted results in every unit, the unit managers and charge nurses socialized it throughout the day every day, and individual coaching was given to everyone who wasn't performing as expected for that particular question.

The results were impressive. The whole time this was in place, scores went up considerably and patient comments reflected that the practice was being done. It was great.

And then…

And then they focused on another question. And guess what happened to the first question. Did those results sustain? Did they continue to do those things they'd been drilled on for weeks before? Nope. They fell off like Humpty Dumpty.

The results for the question they were now focused on were great, just like the first one had been. But those didn't last either. Whatever had the intense focus performed well. Nothing else did.

So I raised my hand and asked, "Can you speak a little about sustainability? When do these behaviors you're coaching for become just part of a normal day, 'this is how we do things here'? Can you explain why they weren't sustained over the long-term?"

They looked at each other for a moment and one of them said, "Well, you know, we ask an awful lot of our nurses. They have so many things they have to focus on; we think we can only ask so much. One thing at a time."

I'm sorry... you got an award for this?

This, in my opinion, is what's wrong with so many hospitals' approaches to improving patient experience. Unless it's part of your culture, unless it's what employees commit to, unless it's "this is how we do things here," you don't have real improvement. You have compliance, but not commitment.

I was so disappointed when I left that session. Any one of us could have given that very same presentation. We have all done that very method of performance improvement and gotten the same results. Why do we keep doing it that way?

It seems that's exactly what so many leadership teams want. They want a spike in improvement that they can show to their bosses. Are we all really that short-sighted? Really? We're celebrating a blip on a spreadsheet. That's just not how I do things. Whenever you have a huge spike, you will have a huge fall. Patient experience is a culture, not a program, and it takes time.

It's time we start rewarding those hospitals that put in the work over the long haul and sustained those improvements over months and years. Let's do it the right way and feature them at the patient experience conferences.

What is your leadership team celebrating?

THE PLATINUM RULE, PART ONE

I, like many of you, was brought up with the Golden Rule: Do unto others as you would have them do unto you or, more simply, treat others as you would like to be treated. There's certainly a lot of good in that rule but I now try to do even better. I try to live by The Platinum Rule: Do unto others as they would like to have done unto them.

I'm not sure who coined the expression, but I first heard it when I was working in Physician Relations at a very large suburban Chicago hospital. None of us in the department was a physician, but we all worked very closely with them and had to continuously find ways to keep them happy, engaged, and admitting their patients to our hospital instead of our competitor down the street.

We all approached the task from our own perspective; what would I want, what would make me happy. A few times we got it right, but if we were going to truly be effective, we had to start seeing things from the physicians' point of view. What would *they* want?

I didn't realize it at the time, but it became a very valuable life lesson for me. I started approaching a lot of things with the Platinum

Rule and it's one of my key points when I'm delivering Patient Experience training.

One of my favorite examples is what to call people. My name, as it appears on my medical chart, is Katherine. But I've found that most people, for some reason, love to use nicknames when they see a long name like Katherine. They call me Kathy. It drives me crazy.

Don't get me wrong, Kathy is a perfectly fine name, it's just not my name and I hate when people assume it's okay to call me that.

Funny thing is, there are Jennifers out there who don't mind being called Jen or Jenny, and Margarets who take it in stride if someone calls them Maggie. These people can't understand why I get so bent out of shape when someone calls me Kathy.

They don't have to understand why. They just have to understand that it does.

So how are you supposed to know? Simple. Ask.

The key to connecting with patients isn't in giving them everything that would make you happy and comfortable if you were in their shoes. We need to ask them what they want.

How many of us actually have a question like that on our admission forms? Or our white boards in patient rooms? We have a perfect opportunity to find out exactly what we can do to make patients' stays with us a little better (and improve our H-CAHPS scores, by the way) and we consistently miss it.

Individualized, personalized care matters. We can't keep going with what we think is important. We have to ask our patients what matters to them and then do it.

It's better than gold; it's platinum.

GOING PLATINUM, PART 2

Last time, I wrote about the Platinum Rule – doing to others as *they* want, not as we want. It's not an easy thing; you have to invest a little energy and ask a person what he or she prefers. Many of us don't feel we have the time, or we assume that others want the same as we do.

I had a friend in college who wanted to do something really wonderful for my birthday so she organized a surprise party for me; secretly invited all my friends, got a big cake, lots of balloons, and many of the foods she'd seen me enjoy. She really did surprise me, too. I had no idea any of it was going on. It was great to see so many people there, all having fun and celebrating. When it came time to blow out the candles, I couldn't believe my eyes. My friend had gotten a chocolate cake. Everyone loves chocolate cake, right?

Not this girl.

I was gracious, smiled, and didn't say anything about it except 'Thank you', but many of my friends gasped when they saw it. "Oh my God, Kate hates chocolate!"

The party went on; I wasn't going to let a little thing like cake ruin it, but it was a perfect example of how we make assumptions about all kinds of things.

We in healthcare do it all the time. This is especially troubling, given all we know about a person's ability to heal and get well.

If I were to ask six different people to tell me the three most important things during their hospital stay, I'd get many different answers. "Manage my pain" "Call me Bill, not William" "Call me Mr. Jones, not Bill" "Please leave the shades closed" "Please always open the shades" "Get me out of here as soon as possible." "Don't send me home before I'm ready" "Communicate with my primary care doctor" and on and on.

We have the perfect opportunity to collect that information. In fact, we have two. There's the admission form when patients first arrive and the white board in their rooms. By simply taking a moment to ask, we can find out what matters most to them. By paying attention to it, we help them get better faster. What better way to demonstrate care and concern that to look at the white board and say, "How are we doing managing your pain today, Mr. Jones? Here, let me open those shades for you."

That simple act, using the Platinum Rule, lets the patient know that we are taking his needs into account. We are personalizing his care. How he feels, what he wants, matters to us.

You don't think you have the time? Believe me, the hospital on the other side of town has already figured this out. They're doing it. They've hardwired it into the behaviors of all the employees who interact with their patients. And patients are noticing. More importantly, they're noticing when it **isn't** happening at your hospital.

Take a few moments to use the Platinum Rule. And please don't bake me a chocolate cake.

PATIENT EXPERIENCE OVER THE HOLIDAYS

I recently traveled back to my hometown of Chicago for a family wedding and made plans to extend my trip a few days to visit with old friends, eat some deep dish pizza, and see the lights along Michigan Avenue and Lake Shore Drive. There's nothing quite like Chicago at Christmastime and seeing my dearest friends did my heart a world of good.

As I was enjoying brunch with one of them, she reminded me that it was five years ago since she had her kidney removed and she'd been cancer-free ever since. I was so happy for her. I don't know a lot of cancer survivors. As a child I'd lost three of my four grandparents to cancer. More recently, I lost my mom to cancer in 2010, my dad to cancer in 2011, and my sister to cancer in 2013. In 2014, this friend of nearly 20 years told me she had cancer. I remember not being able to breathe for several seconds, frightened that I would lose her, too.

A few days before Christmas, she underwent surgery intending to remove just the cancerous section, but once the surgeon was inside, he realized he needed to remove the entire kidney. It was difficult for her to receive that news, but well worth it knowing that it meant a greater chance of her being healthy for years to come.

I really wanted to visit her in the hospital, which wasn't easy with all the craziness of the holiday season, but it turned out that I was able to break away for a bit on Christmas Day. As I pulled into the parking lot that Thursday morning and noticed how many cars weren't there, it struck me that the people who were there as patients must be miserable. Who wants to spend Christmas in the hospital? Even the people working would likely rather be home with their families, right?

She and I had a lovely visit. She didn't look too bad for only being a couple of days post-op, and her spirits were good. I spent about an hour or so with her, until her mom arrived, but was struck at how quiet the hospital was. It was definitely a skeleton crew of clinical staff and not an administrator in sight.

Why would they not have patient advocates or volunteers visiting people that day?

Of course I know why. People don't want to work on holidays and employers don't want to pay hourly employees time-and-a-half to come in. But wouldn't that be a wonderful and meaningful thing to do for patients?

Having a visitor on Christmas Day meant the world to my friend. I think I know what I need to design in my next patient experience director role. Does your hospital have a program like that?

SURPRISE AND DELIGHT

I recently came across a book called The Power of Moments: Why Certain Experiences Have Extraordinary Impact by Chip and Dan Heath. If you haven't read it, I strongly suggest you do. Once I picked it up, I couldn't put it down and it completely changed the way I approach my work in patient experience and employee engagement.

In healthcare, we talk a lot about Evidence-Based Best Practices, things that have been tested and shown to be effective. We work tirelessly to implement and measure best practices and then we wonder why our patient experience scores are so low. It's frustrating.

I took a look at the comments on our surveys and the responses we get on our discharge follow-up phone calls. They largely consist of, "Everything was fine." Ugh. Fine. I hate fine. Fine is the kiss of death.

Turns out, these best practices, things like introducing yourself to patients, explaining what the next steps are in the plan of care, or describing the possible side effects of their medications are things patients have come to expect from us. We're not going to get outstanding surveys if we only give them what's expected. It's like buying a car with air conditioning. We're not going to wow people with the awesome air conditioning package; they expect it. They didn't always. I can still remember cars without air conditioning but it's unthinkable now. Same with these best practices. Patients notice when we *don't* do them.

So how do we create a hospital stay not only memorable enough for patients to bother filling out a survey but also to describe their stay as exceptional?

This is where Dan and Chip's book changed my whole perspective. They dive into the science behind what makes things memorable and offer real-life, practical examples of what staff can do to create those peak moments that patients will remember more than anything else. They don't have to be expensive or labor-intensive or time consuming. They can be quiet moments of connection or surprising moments of responsiveness. And they not only delight the patients, they can touch the other staff, re-engage them, reconnect them to their passion and have a ripple effect across departments.

Best practices are important, they're the minimum level of service we should be providing *every time*, but they're not going to get you anything but middle-of-the-pack results. If you want to deliver a truly exceptional experience, you have to surprise and delight.

The other piece is knowing that, as leaders, we are very good at solving problems. We know how to smooth out the potholes but we probably don't know how to create peak moments for patients. You know who does? Your front line staff, that's who. Let them drive this. Don't roll out some 'moment making' program in which administration tells the staff exactly what they are to do to delight patients. Empower them to come up with those ideas and deliver them.

And while they're out there pouring their hearts into this, you'd better be doing everything you can as a leader to surprise and delight them. Fill their cups, do a few unexpected things to show your support and appreciation of them. Don't expect them to create any moments for patients that you wouldn't also create for them. Watch how fast your culture changes, how happy your staff members are, and how infrequently you hear the words, "Everything was fine," in your discharge follow up phone calls.

PRE-ARRIVAL: BUILDING LOYALTY BEFORE THEY EVEN GET THERE

There are a lot of factors that go into patient loyalty: convenience, location, friendliness, clinical outcomes, but one area that is often overlooked is that of pre-arrival. I saw a study this morning about how pre-arrival is becoming more important to patients than the admission process when answering the question "How likely are you to recommend this hospital?"

This really surprised me, given all the energy we've spent trying to reduce wait times, hire friendly staff, simplify the admission questions, and generally make the process go as quickly and smoothly as possible.

As is often the case in healthcare, I actually realized just how valuable pre-arrival was through my experience with another industry. This past summer, my daughter and I started visiting college campuses. We were planning a trip out west from Chicago and decided to hit four colleges in a week. With plane tickets, hotel stays, rental cars, and mapping everything out online, there was a lot to do and the whole thing was a bit of a blur.

One college really stood out, however. While all of them gave step-by-step directions from the nearest airport to their front door, one had a video. It was shot from the passenger seat of a car and it showed exactly what it looked like while you were heading their way. They zoomed in on the exit signs, let you see just how quickly that right turn that most people miss comes up, showed you where the parking garage was, and then which direction to walk to find the correct building to check in for the tour. It was wonderful.

A few days later while I was driving there, I was comfortable and relaxed. It felt familiar, like I had been there before, even though I hadn't. With all the money hospitals are spending on interior and exterior signage, it's astounding to me that they aren't shooting a video and showing patients what it looks like when you get near their site.

We've become accustomed to using our car's GPS to find a hospital, but what a huge dissatisfier it is to then have no idea where to park, which door to go in, and how to find the registration area. How many front desk receptionists would be delighted to not have to spend the first few minutes of every interaction dealing with angry, frustrated patients and apologizing for the lack of helpful signs or clear directions?

I'm sure more will come out about pre-arrival factors and how they contribute to patient loyalty. This one seems like a good start to me.

What is your hospital doing to make pre-arrival easier for patients?

NINE IMPORTANT THINGS NEW PATIENTS SEE

I recently moved 2000 miles away from the city in which I was born and raised. It was exciting, scary, a little sad, but ultimately a good decision. There are so many things to do when you move across the country; one of them is to find a primary care physician.

Yesterday, I got to see a healthcare system with brand new eyes. I had no preconceived notions about what to expect, I just wanted to find someone close by that looked nice. So, what do new patients actually experience? How do we make them feel good about choosing us?

1. Have a great website. That's where most people go when they're trying to find new health services. There's really only one hospital here, so it wasn't much of a decision, but the physician finder feature on the website was great. I was able to learn a little about each doctor and felt very comfortable with my choice.

2. Have really friendly and knowledgeable people answer the phone. When I called as a new patient, the person on the other end could not have been more helpful.

3. Have some availability in your schedule. I was delighted at how easy it was to get an appointment so quickly.

4. Make your office easy to find. This was one issue I had the day of my appointment. My car's GPS told me I had arrived, but there was no doctor's office around. I called and told them I couldn't find them and the receptionist's directions got me there perfectly. Next time I'll know, but it wasn't obvious to someone unfamiliar with the area.

5. Have an easy check-in process. Again, the front desk staff was great, even with the pile of paperwork to complete.

6. Make sure your medical assistant introduces herself and tells you what's going to happen next. This was textbook perfect. She told me her name, title, every step of the process, which room we were going to, and what she was going to do next.

7. Great bonus – the medical assistant 'managed up' the physician. "You're seeing Dr. M__ today. She is awesome. You'll love her." That was the perfect thing to say to help me relax.

8. Hire physicians who appear to really care about their patients. Not only did this doctor take time to find out what was important to me, she asked that I sit in the comfy chair – not the exam table – so she could look at me and I at her while she was entering all my information into the computer. Nice touch!

9. Leave on a high note. The physician walked me back out to the front desk, where I made another appointment and got

the paperwork for some lab work. The person there gave clear instructions about where to go to get those labs drawn and how quickly I'd get my results. Everyone there thanked me for choosing them and I was on my way.

You never get a second chance to make a first impression and this office did a great job. Have you taken the time to really examine your touchpoints through the eyes of a brand new patient?

Ask someone completely unfamiliar with your hospital or physician office to tell you what their impressions were. You might be surprised at what you take for granted.

SAY HELLO

Shortly after I went to work for a large, multispecialty medical group, I did a little mystery shopping. This group had many locations around town and it was obvious that there was no organization-wide standard for service. Depending on which office you were in, you may be treated beautifully or like an annoyance.

One office in particular I'll never forget. I walked up to the reception desk where a middle-aged woman (that's not a knock; I, too, am a middle-aged woman) was sitting and looking down at some papers. I got to the desk. She looked up at me and didn't say anything. I smiled politely. She raised both eyebrows, made her eyes really big and stuck her neck out a little. I looked at her for another moment before I realized that this was her greeting. She wasn't going to say "Hello" or "How can I help you today". Her idea of a proper greeting in a physician's office was big eyes and a forward neck thrust.

As a perfectly healthy person who was just there to mystery shop and see what was what, I was completely put off. I can only imagine how someone who doesn't feel good and hates going to doctors' offices would react to that kind of first impression.

I don't know what was going on in that woman's life that day, if she'd had a really tough morning and just couldn't force one more smile, if she'd gotten some horrible news, was battling some kind of illness, was thisclose to quitting…

And I didn't care.

Whether we want to admit it or not, healthcare is a service industry. That person behind the desk is an ambassador, a greeter, a tone-setter, a first impression maker, and her personal life must not affect her professional one.

One of the best offices I was ever in had a front desk person who looked genuinely delighted to see every person who came in. Her warm smile and an, "Oh good, it's you!" kind of greeting made everyone feel truly welcome and comfortable. Whether she meant it or not didn't matter. We all believed she did.

Wouldn't you love to be greeted that way?

MANAGE UP

One of my pet peeves (and I have a lot of them) is being led to an exam room by a receptionist who puts me in an exam room, saying, "Someone will be with you shortly."

Someone? Someone who? Who will be with me shortly? I sit and I wait. For someone.

It would be so much nicer if the receptionist said, "Okay, you're going to be right here in exam room 4. Tom will be your medical assistant today and he'll be in to take care of you in just a few minutes. Tom is great. He's one of the best we have here and patients love him. You're in good hands."

Three great things come from those simple words:

1. A nervous patient starts to relax. She has heard that this other care provider is good at his job and is good with patients. She feels better already.

2. Employees actually do a better job after a set of high expectations has been set. I step up my game when I know someone has heard that I'm good at my job. If someone

says I'm warm and friendly, I am turning up the warm and friendly for sure.

3. Co-workers get along better when they get into the habit of speaking well of one another. Less gossip and more praise mean higher morale. And by the way, patients pick up on that, too.

But what are you supposed to do if you're handing a patient off to Tom and you don't like Tom? Do you lie and make something up so the patient feels better? Of course not. Find out a little something about Tom, like how long he's worked here or how many years of experience he has.

Maybe patients like Tom just fine, even if you don't. Try this, "Okay, here we are in room 4. Tom is going to be your medical assistant today. He's been with us for about three years now and patients love him. I'm sure you're going to love him, too. He will be here in just a few minutes."

That wasn't so hard, was it?

And you know, there's a very good chance that after hearing you say nice things about him every day, Tom might actually become easier to work with. You might start to genuinely like him. You'll like coming to work, patients will pick up on the energy and collegiality around the office and nervous patients aren't so nervous anymore.

All because you managed up. What's stopping you?

FINAL IMPRESSIONS

You've got a pet peeve, right? That thing that really irritates you. Nothing huge, just something that gets under your skin.

When it comes to doctor appointments, I think my latest pet peeve is not knowing what to do when you think the visit is over.

It used to be that once you saw the physician and he or she told you what the problem was, a nurse came in to answer any additional questions you might have and told you to check out at the desk before you left the office.

These days, it seems you see the physician, a nurse comes in afterwards to answer any additional questions and tells you to have a nice day. I always find myself stopping at the desk on my way out to be sure there isn't something else I need to do before I go. Usually, the person at the desk is very sweet about it and says something like, "You're all set. Take care!"

Sometimes, though, that person looks really annoyed and says, "Well, did the doctor *say* you needed something else?" in that condescending tone that screams "I hate my job". "No," I reply. "I just wanted to be sure we were good to go," which is often met with a fake, dismissive smile.

And THAT will be my final – and lasting – impression about my visit.

As a Patient Experience trainer, I spend a lot of time talking about the greeting: that first impression that's so important to people when they walk in the door. But lately, I've started spending just as much time on that final acknowledgment, the last thing patients see and hear before they walk out the door. You can undo a lot of good in those final moments, negate the things that had gone well up to that point. Or you can reaffirm your commitment to patient experience and continue to be helpful and kind, even after the visit is over.

The end is just as important as the beginning.

CAN COMPASSION COME IN A POSTCARD?

Anyone who has ever waited for test results to come back knows just how nerve-wracking it can be, especially when it's something you're really concerned about. It may have taken weeks to work up the courage to call and make an appointment and it may have been several more weeks before you actually got in to see a doctor. Those additional few weeks waiting for test results can feel like an eternity.

So when a postcard arrives in the mail with a standard, "Dear Patient, your test results have come back and everything appears to be normal. Please schedule another appointment one year from now," I have to ask: Is this really the best they can do?

I asked a practice manager why her office sends postcards instead of calling patients and her answer was exactly as I imagined, "We're too busy to call every single person. We have to call the ones with bad results because we need to get them back in right away. And the ones with good results always have way too many questions. Our staff simply doesn't have the time."

I was about to start feeling like all was lost, but then I remembered a time, not long ago, when I got a phone call from a physician, not a nurse, not a medical assistant, a *physician* who had test results for me. He called me because he knew I was concerned. He knew I'd been worrying about this the whole time we were waiting. So when he received the faxed results on a Sunday afternoon, he called me himself. I was at a complete loss for words.

Not only was I thrilled at the result, but I was touched that he knew it would mean a lot to hear them from him. He is someone who truly gets it.

Postcards are designed with the staff in mind, not the patient. I realize that time is at a premium and office staff would rather not be on the phone all day, reassuring people that everything's fine. But what a difference it makes. Compassion doesn't come in a postcard.

WHEN YOU SHADOW A DOC

I showed up in the cardiology office at ten minutes to nine that morning, hoping to have a few moments before his first appointment to introduce myself and talk a little bit about why I was there.

Some physicians really hate having someone following them for a few hours and watching everything they do. I'm not sure I'd like it all that much, myself, which is why I like to reassure them that I'm not looking for things to nitpick; I'm there to *say what I see* and help them have better interactions with their patients.

Some are open to the idea. They feel if there's something they can improve, some little thing they can change to connect better with patients, they're willing to listen and let me shadow them for a while.

This was not that kind of day.

The medical assistant walked me back to his office where he was typing some notes into the electronic medical records system. I offered a cheerful, "Good morning," and was ignored. I stood in the doorway and waited for him to finish. He looked up, "You here to see me?"

I introduced myself and as soon as I said "service excellence department" he cut me off. "So you're going to be following me around this morning? Alright, let's get started." He walked down the hall into the exam room. And just like that, I had lost control of the interaction.

With no real introduction of who I was, no knowledge of my background, experience, what my intentions were, and not even a suggestion of how to introduce me to his patients, he opened the exam room door, said hello to his patient and told her he had someone following him around today. I smiled warmly at the patient to reassure her and tried not to let my discomfort show.

All morning, he went from room to room, patient to patient, without any breaks in between, making it impossible for me to speak to him. At one point, he told a patient that he was being watched by the quality department today and "that's what you get when you're working for the man." A chuckle from him at the end of that sentence would have eased some of the tension, but it never came.

At noon, he told me he was headed to lunch and any feedback I had for him, I could send in an email. Before I could answer, he turned and headed down the stairwell. Gone.

I stood there for a few moments, wondering how, in all my years of experience, I had let this happen. The answer came to me sometime later: I'd had a number of really wonderful interactions with others in that department. Physicians, Nurse Practitioners, and Physician Assistants who were very happy to have someone come and help them out. This was an office that was incentivized based, in part, on their patient experience scores and the group really wanted to perform well. Everyone up to that point had been looking for someone to help them get better. I assumed he was of the same mind. Boy, was I wrong.

The lesson for me here, clearly, was never, ever assume. Never think you can skip over the fundamentals of a proper introduction, building rapport, and discussing your feelings about both shadowing and being shadowed. It's a sensitive thing for some people, so just a few moments of talking ahead of time can make all the difference.

WHEN LEADERS ROUND
ON STAFF

It was still dark when my alarm went off. I got out of bed, stumbled into the shower, managed to find clothes that matched, and headed to the hospital to round on some staff members in the middle of the night.

One of the things my former health system did is get leadership to get out on the floors, into all the departments, and talk to staff. The goal was to find out what's working well, what we could be doing better to support them in their work, be visible, approachable, and make connections.

I got to the hospital and was struck by how quiet it was. Usually when I got to work there was a lot going on, people everywhere, visitors trying to find patient rooms, lots of commotion. Now, it was quiet and I didn't see anyone as I came in through the employee entrance and made my way to my office to drop off my things.

I headed up to one of the nursing units I visited on a daily basis. I knew just about everyone on the day shift and looked forward to seeing them each day. That night, I met people I'd never met before. People who were incredibly dedicated to their jobs. People who had worked there for more than 25 years. People who truly believed in the mission.

They didn't know me, but they opened up to me, told me what they loved about working there, what they wished we would change, what we as leaders could do to help them be more effective. It was eye-opening, amazing, and humbling.

I met an RN who told me that "Christmas came early" because we approved a position that gave him additional support overnight and relieved him of the stress he'd been feeling. I spoke to a nursing assistant who said she felt like this was a second home to her because of her fabulous teammates.

And I never would have met them had I not signed up to do leader rounding.

Leader rounding is an evidence-based practice that increases not only direct-care staff engagement but leader engagement, as well.

When we get out from behind our desks and talk to people, it improves staff morale and helps us feel more a part of things. Talking to people you don't normally talk to or even see is a great way to understand what's really going on.

If you're a leader, get out there and round. If you're a direct-care worker, talk to the leaders when they come to your unit or department. Tell them what you love and what you wish they'd improve. We're listening.

THE CASE FOR LEADER ROUNDING

They call it sacred time. That hour between 9 and 10am where the leaders of the hospital go into their assigned rooms out on the floors and talk to patients and their families. It's an hour when no meetings are to be scheduled. It's protected time, dedicated solely to patient rounds.

Sometimes it's a social visit: how are things going, is there anything we can do to improve your stay, do you need anything, etc. Sometimes, it's a focus on a particular issue: is it quiet at night, are you able to get enough rest, what kind of noise is keeping you awake, is it equipment, staff, other patients?

After rounding, there's a huddle to review any big issues that need escalation and recognize any staff that patients said provided outstanding care and service. It becomes very apparent at those huddles who is doing those rounds and who is phoning it in. When day after day, a person says, "My patients were sleeping," or "My patients said everything was fine," we know there's not a whole lot of quality rounding going on.

It was a source of frustration for me, trying to make those leaders understand the importance of connecting with patients. After all, this was our opportunity to see the hospital through their eyes and find out what's working well, what's not, and what's important to them so we could make things better. Why wouldn't they make time for that?

Pleading and begging and even data about how leader rounds improves patient experience scores didn't appear to be having much of an impact. Turns out, nothing is as compelling as a real-life story.

David was in charge of facilities, a no nonsense kind of guy who made sure all the engineering, heating and cooling, and equipment was humming. I never would have guessed he'd be so passionate about patient care.

He was in a room one morning trying to have a conversation with the patient and his family members and needed an interpreter. We had interpreter services with an outside company and, while reaching those individuals was sometimes a chore, it was necessary. After connecting with them, it was clear the family was in the dark about what was happening when the physicians and nurses came in.

David hung in there. He stayed with them, wanting to know if they knew what the patient's condition was, if they understood what the medications were for, if they'd had a chance to ask questions, and on and on. He reassured them, told them he'd get them the answers they needed and left to find the manager of the unit.

She, too, did some digging and identified each of the nurses who had been caring for this family. Of the six or seven, only one had documented in the chart that she had used the language assistance program.

From that moment on, everything changed with this family. No one went into that patient's room without the interpreter service and no one left without checking with the family that all of their questions were answered.

We likely never would have known any of this without the leader rounding program and for David's persistence. He could have reported that the patient wasn't English speaking and the interpreter services weren't working. He could have reported that the family said everything was fine. He could have skipped the room altogether and just said the patient was sleeping, But he didn't. He went in, took the time, and helped this family get answers.

I can only imagine what they must have been feeling until David stepped in.

Some hospitals don't do leader rounding because they think it's too much work or they don't want the nurses to think they're checking up on them. We do it because we feel that leaders are part of the care team. We bring a different perspective in with us and we're another set of eyes making sure patients and their families are receiving the best possible care and service.

David's story was just what we needed to light a fire under some of the leaders and help them see just how important it is. I hope it does the same for you.

MORE ON DAILY ROUNDING

"Thank you for coming back and checking on me."

For years, the patient experience experts have been touting the benefits of daily rounds on patients by members of the leadership staff. I don't think anyone would disagree that it's good for leaders to get out from behind their desks and out on the floors. Staff appreciate seeing executives up close and patients feel good knowing that the leaders of the hospital are involved in the day-to-day goings on.

I had always worked in hospitals that were so large that rounding on 100% of patients every day wasn't the expectation. We encouraged people to do "as many as they could" and hoped they got to maybe half. In fact, one hospital had a goal of 4 patients per unit per day. In a 54-bed unit, it felt like we were sending a clear message that it didn't really matter.

Currently, I work in a health system that expects leader rounding on 100% of patients every day and there are processes in place to ensure it's happening. Like many non-clinical leaders, I was apprehensive about going into a patient room for a quick visit. Normally, when I get called to visit a patient, it's because he or she is upset about something and I'm there to try and solve a specific problem. Without a task to accomplish, what would we talk about?

Well, there are some general questions we ask to get the conversation started and it was surprising to me just how much people want someone to talk to when they're stuck in a hospital bed all day. I thought they'd shoo me away and ask to be left alone so they could sleep but almost everyone has been happy to spend a few moments chatting about how their stay has been.

Additionally, it's been very rewarding to visit the same people a few days in a row and see their faces light up when I walk into the room. "Oh, hi! You're back."

I had visited one woman every morning for the past three days and really enjoyed her. She was in a fair amount of pain but kept in good spirits by watching Christmas movies on the Hallmark channel. She told me about her kids, her grandchildren, her recent health problems, and all the things she hoped to do once she got home.

Our rounding time is set to happen between 9-10am, but after visiting with her one morning, I learned she was scheduled for some surgery later in the day. I maneuvered some things around in my calendar and decided to go back up afterwards to see how she was doing. She was genuinely happy to see me and I her.

We spent only a short time together but it was good to see that she had gotten through the procedure just fine. As I got up and headed for the door, she said, "Thank you for coming back and checking on me."

Leader rounding is certainly beneficial to patients, but it can also be beneficial to us if we approach it with the intention of making a meaningful connection instead of simply checking the box and saying, "Yep, I went in there. Everything's fine."

Keep in mind, too, that bedside nurses notice when we come back outside of the designated rounding time. Instead of simply doing exactly what's expected of us and nothing more, we can demonstrate genuine patient care and role model going above and beyond by popping in throughout the day.

For any executive who says, "I don't have time," I encourage you to make time. Block out 30 minutes as sacred time when meetings cannot be scheduled. Get out from behind your desk and spend some time with the staff and a couple of patients. It's good for them and good for you, too.

THE NO PASS ZONE PITFALL

In every hospital I've ever worked, we've observed something called the No Pass Zone. The No Pass Zone means that when a call light is on outside a patient's room, whoever is nearby, no matter what their job title, stops and answers the light. We go in, we tell the patient we saw the call light was on, and we ask what we can do to help.

No exceptions. You do not walk past a patient room when a light is on. Ever.

We drill this like crazy at new employee orientation. We tell clinical and non-clinical staff alike, "Do not walk past a room if there's a light on. It doesn't matter if that's not your patient or you're not an RN, or you're in a hurry. If a light is on, you go in." It's crystal clear.

So what could possibly go wrong?

I was on my way up to the 3rd floor one Thursday morning to do my daily patient rounds. Each of us on the leadership team has an assignment of four patient rooms to round on. We ask questions about their stay, like which staff member can we recognize for doing a great job, what can we be doing differently to make the stay with us a little better, and some focus questions about a specific topic we're trying to measure, like quiet and restfulness or RN Communication.

I got off the elevator with my rounding questions all ready to go when the very first room down the corridor had its call light on.

My eyes locked in on that soft white glow hanging from the ceiling. I could see nothing else. This was it. This was my moment. I was going to answer a call light. My mother, an RN of nearly 50 years, would be so proud.

I went into the room and saw a face that was familiar to me. He was a patient from a few weeks ago who had been in one of my assigned rooms for several days; I'd gotten to know him a bit. He looked different today.

"Hi!" I said. "I remember you! I saw your light on, how can I help you?"

"I need my nurse," he cried. "My stomach is in so much pain and I just pooped myself and I called the nurse and I need help!"

"Oh my... okay... I'll find your nurse... hang on... I'll get some help."

I ran out into the hallway and saw the manager of the unit. "Hey," I said, "I answered the call light in room 301. The patient said he pooped himself and needs his nurse."

She looked at me and said very calmly, "Okay, Kate, I'll get his nurse. You know you were just in a room with a patient who has C-diff, right?"

I stopped dead in my tracks. "What?" C.-diff is clostridium difficile, a nasty little bug that wreaks havoc on your colon.

"Kate, go wash your hands with soap and water. Didn't you see the signs on the door about contact precautions or notice the cart with all the PPE on it?"

Actually, no. I hadn't.

Right outside the room there was a cart with PPE – personal protective equipment – gowns, gloves, and masks and a big sign, warning that we needed to take precautions before entering. I was so fixated on the call light, I never saw them.

Thankfully, I hadn't actually touched anything in the room, but I still felt like I had cooties all over me. I washed my hands for what seemed like an hour.

Here's the thing: depending on our lens, we tend to fixate on certain things. As the patient experience director and a non-nurse, when I saw a call light, all I could think to do was answer it. Immediately. Someone needs help. Go help.

What we can't forget to do is pause and take a look around. Notice the big red signs on the door. As you walk around the giant cart of PPE to get to the door, stop for a second and ask yourself why it's there. Don't get so caught up in your own forest that you can't see the other trees.

THE ELEPHANT IN THE ED

I am a big fan of Liz Jazwiec and her 2009 book Eat That Cookie! Make Workplace Positivity Pay Off for Individuals, Teams and Organizations. In it, she talks of her time as the manager of a busy Chicago emergency department where the motto seemed to be "I'm here to save your ass, not kiss it."

I first heard of Liz when the hospital I was working for at the time hired her to give a talk to our managers and directors. She had been a patient experience cynic who thought the whole thing was ridiculous. The president of her hospital told her she had to get her patient experience scores up or she'd be looking for another job. At first, she resisted but soon realized he was serious.

Like so many nurse managers I've met, she thought patient experience was fluff stuff and had no place in healthcare, especially a busy ED where things were quite literally life and death. She sneered at the smile police who told her to "just be nice" while she was working hard to bring people back from the brink of death.

To Liz, many of her patients were cranky, ungrateful whiners who were tough to deal with. But as she started being nicer, she was surprised that they started being less cranky, showed some appreciation, and were easier to deal with.

Eventually, Liz not only got her patient experience scores up, she became a believer in the patient experience movement, even becoming a coach for The Studer Group. I love her story and if you haven't read her book, you really should.

Something else to consider when it comes to the ED is throughput and the effect it has on the nurses.

Much of the patient dissatisfaction in the ED comes from waiting too long with no idea of what's happening and why. Staff can certainly help by keeping patients informed but when things are backed up, staff start feeling the pressure, too. When there's no available bed on the floor, an ED nurse has to be a telemetry nurse, something they don't particularly enjoy.

ED nurses are trained to stabilize and either discharge or admit. Once the decision has been made, the ED nurse moves on to the next patient. To have a bunch of patients on gurneys lining the hallway needing ongoing care makes ED nurses anxious. They want the patients to get up to the floors as much as the patients do.

Additionally, there are patients in the ED who need specialized care that the hospital may or may not provide. Sometimes, getting a surgeon or psychiatrist to come in can be a challenge and getting a patient transferred to another facility can take hours. These situations, too, can make staff anxious; they have to manage the questions and complaints but they're powerless to actually fix them.

Without efficient discharge processes on the floors, patients can end up staying a day or two longer than needed and that means longer waits in the emergency department for patients who need an inpatient bed. Case managers, social workers, hospitalists, attending physicians, and house supervisors all play a role that affects wait times, and, subsequently, patient experience in the ED.

Nothing can take the place of a warm greeting, staff that meet and even anticipate your needs, and physicians that explain things in a way you can understand. But when it comes to patient satisfaction in the ED, you have to include throughput and inpatient discharge processes in your efforts or you're only solving part of the problem.

THE PATIENT
EXPERIENCE TEAM

A while back, I was invited to be part of a team designed to improve the experience of our patients in the Emergency Department. It was a multidisciplinary team made up of physicians, nurses, techs, security, people from the lab, security, and of course, the department of patient experience.

At the first meeting, we talked about our scope, the projects we want to tackle, the metrics we'd use to measure our success, how often we'd meet..., all of that important stuff.

We had a few people focusing on workflow efficiencies and how we could streamline some of our processes so that patients were seen quicker.

We had some people focus on inter-departmental communication. When nursing asks imaging to do or change something, how does it impact that department? How should physicians be interacting with techs? What kinds of communication styles are most effective in an emergency department setting?

We had a small team focused on staff resilience and how to not let one mean patient ruin your whole shift. They found ways to give nurses 15 minutes to collect themselves after a bad interaction so they could meet the next patient with kindness.

We had a person (me) focused on training staff on communication, specifically compassion, de-escalation, and empathy. We role-played, we practiced managing-up our colleagues, and made sure all the staff went through the 3-hour training.

We thought we had all our bases covered. But no one on this team was assigned to deal with tactical patient needs.

We knew that one of our biggest issues was keeping patients informed of wait times. Do you think we remembered to create a designated group of people to go out every 20-30 minutes and talk to people in the waiting room about how much longer it would be and offer them something like a pillow or blanket while they waited? Nope.

We got so focused on the big picture stuff – processes, efficiencies, training, etc., we completely forgot about the little things – acts of kindness to our patients – things that often make the biggest difference.

When you're working on improving the patient experience, don't forget about the patients.

VOICE OF THE PATIENT

One of the best things you can do to enhance your patient experience program is to involve patients and their families in hospital committees and utilize their feedback and suggestions. I've been fortunate in my career to have created Patient and Family Advisory Councils in four different organizations. What I learned from them was incredibly valuable.

The first one was a Donor Family Advisory Council at the Chicago-based organ procurement organization. I was heading up the Family Support Services department and we wanted to find more and better ways to care for families after they'd made the decision to donate a loved one's organs for transplant. Although I'd worked with hundreds of families and helped them with that decision, I had never actually experienced it first-hand.

The simple question, "How could we have made this process easier for you?" opened my eyes to just what it was these families went through as they struggled with the decision. Additionally, they offered suggestions for follow-up once the decision was made, things they wanted to know about the process, and ways our organization could honor their loved one years later.

The next one was at a large, independent multi-specialty medical group. The questions I asked were more about their visit to the doctor's office, ease of scheduling, cleanliness of the facility, the friendliness of staff and how well the doctor listened to them. There, we got some great insight as to just how difficult it can be to find the office when the signage isn't very clear, how long patients actually wait in the waiting room before seeing their physician, and the things they overhear the staff saying when they think no one can hear them. Very eye-opening.

The third and fourth were at large independent hospitals in different parts of the country where our main focus was on inpatient stays. The council gave us feedback on both the clinical and non-clinical staff, things they wished we would have done for them while they were staying with us, way-finding around our hallways, and billing frustrations. These were all things I had brought to administration, but having the voice of the patients behind me gave it more credibility, more weight.

Engaging with patients who had some not-so-great experiences with your organization is humbling, but so important if you really want to improve. When I can bring an issue to an executive committee and tell them, "This is what our patients are saying," they listen.

If you don't currently have a patient advisory council, you really should. They take time and energy to get started and maintain but provide an invaluable service. They can serve as ambassadors to the community, spreading the word about the programs and services you offer, they can shine a light on blind spots, uncover problems you may not know existed, and offer solutions you may never have thought of.

What to know what patients want? Involve them.

THE TROUBLE WITH HCAHPS

"I had no idea. We're actually doing a lot better
than I thought we were."

I've always struggled with the way HCAHPS scores are presented. The grids that the big patient satisfaction vendors produce show the percentage of patients who gave the very best score (we call that Top Box), and where that percentage ranks among your peers. Let's say 80% of your patients say the nurses *always* treated them with courtesy and respect. Depending on how patients in other hospitals rate the nurses, that 80% could put you in the 95th percentile or the 30th. It's all about the compare group.

When the percentile rank is the only thing staff see, they don't really have a good sense of just how well or poorly they're doing. They don't know if the other 20% of patients are saying the nurses *usually*, *sometimes*, or *never* treated them with respect, but it makes a big difference.

I was presenting the latest patient experience data to our nurse leaders, many of whom were new to their role, only this time, I didn't give them the prefabricated grid that showed our percentile ranking.

They'd seen that grid over and over and all it did was frustrate and demoralize. "How could we be in the 12th percentile? I know we have great nurses here."

Instead, I took the distribution of responses (Strongly Agree, Agree, Disagree, Strongly Disagree) to the question Would you Recommend this Hospital to Your Friends and Family and put those in a pie chart. I called their attention to the percentage of Strongly Agree and Agree responses and showed them that the overwhelming majority of our patients have a positive reaction to us. We weren't horrible. We weren't delivering terrible care to our patients.

For months, staff saw our very low ranking and thought we were miles away from our goal of the 75th percentile. The scores were meaningless because the goal seemed completely unattainable. Showing them this distribution of scores reinvigorated them.

- If we can just move the second highest score to the highest score, we'll be in fantastic shape.

- Patients aren't perceiving us as bad nurses, we just have to be more consistent in our delivery of care.

- If it only takes one person dropping the ball for that rating to go from *always* to *usually*, don't be that one person.

These were things staff could wrap their minds around. So if you have to present HCAHPS scores, present them in a different way, a way that doesn't frustrate, depicts the human story behind the score, makes the goal appear within reach, and illustrates just how directly staff influence those scores. It may be the first time they've ever heard them that way.

WHAT DOES THAT SCORE MEAN?

I've worked in patient experience for many years in several organizations in different parts of the country and, while there are differences between health systems, there's one thing I've seen in every one of them: a firm belief that only the angry people fill out surveys.

It simply isn't true.

And it makes me sad because it tells me that no one has taken the time to really explain these scores.

Typically, when scores are posted, staff only see their percentile ranking. This is how your hospital compares to the rest of the hospitals in the database. It's important because this is how CMS determines your reimbursement, but it doesn't tell the whole story.

One of the best things you can do, especially in an under-performing hospital, is to break down the percentage of patients' ratings for each question. If you're scoring low when you look at the percentile ranking, look instead at how you're actually being rated.

For example, in answer to the question "Would you recommend this hospital to your friends and family?" your hospital's responses are:

Definitely Yes 66%

Probably Yes 23%

Probably No 8%

Definitely No 3%

Does that look like only the angry people are filling out surveys? 89% of patients would recommend you. That looks pretty good, right?

Here's the thing: CMS is only looking at the percentage of patients that gave you the highest, or Top Box, response. If it isn't Definitely Yes, it doesn't count. And, they're comparing you to the other hospitals in the country and right now, 66% only puts you at about the 35th percentile.

Think of it this way: if I got a 66% on a math test in a class full of smart kids who all got 90% and my teacher *grades on a curve,* I just failed. But if I'm in a class full of knuckleheads who all got 30%, I got an A. It's all about your compare group. And you can't control your compare group.

For a hospital that's low in the percentile rankings, I find it's best to break out each of the responses and focus on moving the second-highest scores to the Top Box scores.

Here's another example: your score for courtesy and respect for nursing is in the 12th percentile. Sounds terrible, right? But if you break it out, it might look something like this:

"During this hospital stay, how often did the nurses treat you with courtesy and respect?"

Always 70%

Usually 24%

Sometimes 4%

Never 2%

94% of patients gave positive responses; the key is in moving people from Usually to Always.

When I took this approach and broke it down to the staff, a huge lightbulb went on and suddenly, it all started to make sense. Now, they weren't feeling defeated being in the 12th percentile. Now, they knew they had to move a few Usually responses to Always responses and they didn't have that far to go.

I still would want to investigate the 2% of patients who said Never, but the message to the staff, the way to keep them engaged and excited is to show them they're not doing nearly as bad as they think and that it isn't only the angry people who fill out surveys.

YES, WE SURVEY THE ANGRY PEOPLE

Last time, I wrote about patient experience scores, the percentile rankings, the distribution of responses, and how staff are almost always surprised when they see that it isn't just the angry people who fill out surveys. One thing that inevitably gets asked whenever I present this kind of data is, "Can we filter out the people who leave here ticked off so they don't get a survey?"

I used to laugh when they'd ask that, but quickly realized they weren't joking. They'd really like us to exclude dissatisfied people. But it doesn't work that way.

Let's start with the obvious. Really? You *really* want us to **not** get feedback from people unless they're happy? Does any company have that luxury? With Yelp just a click away, every business is subject to ratings, good and bad. I can rate everything from my dinner at the four-star restaurant to the Uber driver who took me there. If they want good reviews, they need to do a good job, not cherry pick the satisfied customers. That's not just dishonest, it's silly, as it sets a completely unrealistic set of expectations. It would be even more disappointing to have a bad experience because, according to the reviews, no one has ever had a bad experience.

But more importantly, we learn more from our unhappy patients than we do from our happy ones. As much as I tend to focus on the positive, there are often ideas or suggestions from patients who wanted something more from us that are really constructive and useful.

For example, at one hospital, we added some simple signage in our parking garage to more clearly point out the entrance for day-surgery patients. At another, we created scripting for our medical assistants that let patients know they could skip the checkout desk unless they needed a follow-up appointment. These were things that were easy to address but, had it not been for the surveys, we wouldn't have realized they were dissatisfiers.

And most of us have a blind spot about our own words and actions. I've known plenty of people (myself included) who say things with the best of intentions, not realizing they're annoying or downright offensive to some people. This is especially true in healthcare settings where people tend to be a bit more sensitive. But how else would we know if we didn't receive the feedback?

Let me be quick to say that it's equally important to celebrate and recognize the positive comments that come through on those surveys. People love to know that their hard work doesn't go unnoticed or unappreciated, and it's a great way to improve your organization's culture. But it's a mistake to not look at ways you can make things even better.

Yes, it's discouraging to see negative comments, especially when you remember that particular patient and you remember doing everything you could to try and make their visit a pleasant one. But any organization (or individual for that matter) that wants to improve should hear some honest feedback, even if it's tough to take. Surrounding yourself with people who never complain or offer some constructive criticism won't help you get any better.

WHO IS HEALED BY
HEALING ARTS?

Part of one of my former roles within the health system was to over-see the Healing Arts program. It included music, visual art, gardens, and even visits from dogs. There was a grand piano in the front entrance of the main hospital with a lot of additional open space which allowed for all kinds of musicians to come and play. There have been string quartets, harps, flautists, and full orchestras, and no matter what the style of music, I always saw people stopping for a few moments to listen. Visitors, patients or staff, people really seemed to appreciate it when there was music in the lobby.

It was not uncommon for me to receive a phone call from someone who wanted to play our piano, but there's a reason we kept it locked. Our players were vetted; they needed to audition and undergo a background check before we let them play. There's an integrity to the program I wanted to preserve. Few things are more annoying than hearing a toddler bang on the keyboard or a young kid in his second year of lessons plunk out the first few measures of "Fur Elise." Even those who are pretty decent players occasionally forget that this is a hospital, not an amphitheater. You need to watch the volume and be mindful of your song selection. It's part of a healing ministry, not a concert.

So a few months into the job, I got a call from a woman whose son was a patient and would be there for quite some time. She felt it would be very healing for her to be able to play while she was in town visiting him. I tried to explain the program to her and how it wasn't really designed for people to just drop in and start playing. She kept telling me how much it would help her cope with this extraordinarily stressful situation but I told her no. I couldn't let her play.

A day or so later, I got an email from her daughter, pleading her case. She insisted her mom was classically trained and had played for years and we should really make an exception for her. I again responded with, "I'm so sorry, but no."

About a week later, the patient himself, who was well enough to walk around the hospital but not well enough to go home, found my office. He told me I was doing an incredible disservice not only to his mother but to our visitors and staff who were being robbed of the chance to hear his mom play. He told me I was failing at my job by not having enough music in our lobby and not allowing people to share their gifts.

Flustered and feeling completely defensive, I agreed to let her play.

An hour later, mom was in my office with her music books. We went to the piano and she started to play some Chopin. It was quite nice. She then pulled out a Scott Joplin book of ragtime. Now, having taken a few years of piano lessons, myself, I can tell you that ragtime is tough. Really tough. Lots of notes and it needs to be played at a quick tempo to sound good. She missed a few notes and each time, she made an 'oops' face or said, "Sorry!" I was willing to let her limp along for one song, but when she started in on another, I had to intervene.

"Are you comfortable playing that style of music?"

She stopped, closed the book and said, "Well I'm really out of practice. It's been three weeks since I've played." I told her the Chopin was lovely and asked if she had any others like that. She scrunched her face into a frown and answered, "I know those. I need to practice the Scott Joplin."

And that's when I realized I should have stuck to my guns.

The piano in the lobby isn't there for musicians to practice on. The person who donated it didn't do it so that people in the community could work on their fingering or practice their scales. Its primary purpose is to bring joy and comfort to the people listening. It's a lovely secondary gain when it also brings joy and comfort to the players.

I certainly didn't make a friend that day. Not only was the woman upset with me, her children were, too, but intention means a lot to me. If you're there to play because you want to share your gifts and make others happy, you are welcome to play. If you're there for you; to practice, to make yourself feel better or simply to show off, please go to a rehearsal room, somewhere other than a hospital. The Healing Arts program is for the artists who are there to help others heal.

PX MASTERMIND

This past week, I was invited to lead a Patient Experience Mastermind webinar on Best Practices and Lessons Learned.

I love that there is a vibrant and passionate community of PX professionals who are continuously learning and sharing their experiences with one another. I was honored to share what I know but even more excited at the idea of learning from the others on the call.

This was a huge topic so I broke it down into three major categories: Leadership, Data, and Originality. The first two are things I hear being brought up all the time. Culture change doesn't happen without a firm commitment from leaders and a shared vision across the organization. And there are many more sources of data than simply the H-CAHPS scores. We spoke about all the ways patients and their families tell us about their experiences, yet we only seem to focus on a single number reported monthly.

That third category, originality, is where I spent the most time. There are all kinds of new innovations out there, new tech designed to deliver the ultimate patient experience, new philosophies about doing WITH our patients instead of doing TO or FOR them, and even a hospital offering a money back guarantee if you're unhappy with your service. There are new ways of executing old ideas: rounding with an iPad instead of paper and pen, putting your patient and family advisory council members on hospital committees, and moving physicians from 'on-board' to actively leading your PX efforts.

The other piece of originality is you. Your personal and professional experiences, along with your natural talents and abilities, all inform your approach to this kind of work. While I love that we can share and learn from each other, we need to bring our authentic selves and not rely on scripting or a cookie cutter formula for success.

Let's continue to talk about best practices and share our ideas. Let's talk about approaches that worked and those that didn't work. And let's not forget who we are, what we bring, how we feel, and why we do this. Our patients and their families will love us for it.

SECTION THREE:
THE STAFF STORIES

This is really where it starts and ends, you know; with the staff. How we select them, how we train them, how we grow and develop them, how we reward and celebrate them, how we counsel and coach them. They are the ones who have to execute on leadership's plans. They are the face of our hospital. They're pretty important.

Most people, when asked why they stay in a particular job for so long, will tell you it's because they love their co-workers. We spend more waking hours with them than we do our own families, don't we? One Debbie Downer can ruin your whole department.

Once you've hired right, you need a really good on-boarding and training program. Goals, expectations, processes, systems; a new person has a lot to learn and a comprehensive program will give them the confidence they need to do good work.

Finally, you need leaders that empower their teams. Empowered employees are happy employees. I love that a Chief Nurse Executive said to me that everyone in her hospital was empowered to exceed patient expectations. No one had to ask permission or send a bunch of emails to get approval in order to do something special for a patient. How refreshing!

It was no surprise to me that her hospital was one of the best-performing in the country.

Enjoy The Staff Stories.

THE PATIENT
EXPERIENCE NURSE

Earlier this month, we celebrated Nurse's Week. Our Chief Nurse Executive had a whole week of wonderful things planned for the department including massages, root beer floats, a homemade meatball contest, and an awards ceremony. She had a few different categories but the one that caught my attention was the Patient Experience Award, given to the nurse who consistently exemplified excellent patient experience.

The winner was someone I knew. I had spoken with him a time or two when I did patient rounds on his floor and had heard his name a lot as someone patients absolutely loved. The next time I saw him, I pulled him aside to congratulate him and I asked him what it was he did that earned him this award.

"I just talk to them."

"Come on, James," I said. "Lots of nurses talk to patients. What are you doing that's making such a difference?"

His answer was not what I was expecting. I thought he'd go into some big thing about how he always does AIDET when he's in a patient room and he always calls them by the name they wish to be called and he always manages up the other staff... Nope.

"I believe it's my job to help them understand their disease so they can better manage it," he said. "Most of them don't connect the dots between what they do and how they feel. If I can help them see how doing this thing makes them sick, they're less likely to do that thing. If they understand that their health is something they can control, they usually do. But, too often, they come in, they get some meds, they go home, and then they're right back here again in a few weeks. I want to change that. I talk to them. I work with them. I encourage them. I help them."

"Wow," I answered. "That was not what I thought you were going to say."

"I can see myself in everyone here. You got your life together? Great, me too. You got problems? Things in your life went sideways? I get it. I was there, too. You can't judge people. If you judge, you can't understand. If you understand, you can't judge. You just talk to them so they know you're on their side, you're rooting for them. I think that's what I do."

I thanked him and left feeling so good that we had someone like that working at our hospital. Maybe that's the secret sauce, someone who connects with, roots for, and educates patients. Someone who doesn't judge, but listens, informs, cares. Do you have a James at your hospital?

APPRECIATIVE COACHING

What's the best way to help people improve? How do we work with staff members who do a good job and help them get even better?

Many of us came into leadership positions at a time when we focused on the gaps: what our employees needed to work on and where they were weakest. During annual evaluations, we centered the discussion around mistakes and weaknesses.

There's a better way.

Appreciative coaching focuses on what people are doing well. It allows them to determine where they'd like to improve.

For example, when watching a nurse do hourly rounding, we might say, "I observed your interaction with Mrs. Jones. How do you think it went? I saw you do __ and __ really well, great job! What do you think could have gone better? Okay, how can I help you with that?"

When we use appreciative coaching, four things happen:

1. **We build a road to improvement.** Employees are more likely to make improvements when they identify the things

they want to do better. We tend to follow through on things when they're our own ideas.

2. **We make it 'safe' to not be perfect** as long as we're still trying. Employees do better when they're supported, not criticized.

3. **We foster a culture of recognition and appreciation.** When we tell employees what they're good at and how important those skills are, they do them more often and even better than before.

4. **As leaders, we start to see our staff differently.** When we look for the good, we tend to see more good.

Of course, if there are some serious performance issues, that's an entirely different conversation. But for your high-performing staff, try a little appreciative coaching.

MORE THOUGHTS ON APPRECIATIVE COACHING

Last time, I wrote about appreciative coaching and how it's more effective for people to improve and learn. Well, this past week, quite by accident, I stumbled upon an article from the Harvard Business Review entitled "Why Feedback Fails." In studying how people learn, thrive, and excel, they point to three core evidence-based learning theory tenets:

1. Telling people what we think of their performance doesn't help them thrive and excel, and telling people how we think they should improve actually *hinders* learning;

2. Humans are highly unreliable raters of other humans. The feedback you give is more about you than the person receiving the feedback;

3. The only realm in which humans are an unimpeachable source of truth is that of their own feelings and experiences.

   People tend to perform better by being given goals and results to achieve, when they receive positive feedback about what they are doing well, and by watching other people excel and receive validation for their excellence. The article went so far as to give examples on how to more effectively communicate with teams to elicit these principles:

Instead of: Try:

Can I give you some feedback?	Here's my reaction
Good job!	Here are three things that really worked for me. What was going through your mind when you did them?
Here's what you should do	Here's what I would do
Here's where you need to improve	Here's what worked best for me and why
That didn't really work	When you did (x) I felt (y) – or – That didn't really work for me
You need to improve your communication skills	Here's exactly where you started to lose me
You need to be more responsive	When I don't hear from you, I worry we're not on the same page
You lack strategic thinking	I'm struggling to understand your plan
You should do _____ (in response to being asked for advice)	What do you feel you're struggling with and what have you done in a similar situation?

You might find that you've done a few things in the left col-
umn. That's okay. We all have. But now we know better. Modeling
and recognizing excellence is more effective in helping teams provide excellent care, everytime.

Reference: Marcus Buckingdall and Ashley Goodall. "The Feedback Fallacy."
Harvard Business Review, March-April 2019 edition. https://hbr.org/2019/03/
the-feedback-fallacy

I SAID WHAT?

Patients hear everything.

Whether they're in a physician office, an imaging center, or a hospital, they hear just about everything we say to each other.

In every hospital I've worked in, we've told staff that their personal conversations belong in the break room, not outside patient rooms, and, for the most part, they've done a good job of keeping the stories of their latest private adventures off the floor.

Here's what we didn't expect: nurses do a lot of talking about patients' bowel movements and dressing changes and patients are just as put off hearing about those things as they are about your date last weekend. While they understand things like that need to be discussed, many of them told us they came to know other patients by their bathroom habits and it was unsettling.

Most of the time, however, patients are listening to what we're saying to each other about each other.

Although it was years ago, I remember like it was yesterday waiting in my doctor's office and overhearing the front desk staff say to one another, "Oh, stay away from Dr. X today. He's in a bad mood." I was waiting to see Dr. X and I couldn't help but worry that he'd snap at me, try to rush me out, or roll his eyes if I asked a question. He didn't. He treated me just as he'd done every time before, but hearing that statement caused all kinds of unnecessary anxiety. Not only should I not have heard it for my sake, but for Dr. X's. A new patient might have gotten a very different impression of him based on what they'd overheard.

And in an inpatient unit where they may have limited mobility, patients often feel anxious about the kind of care they're going to receive. When they hear us speaking unfavorably about the physicians or the other nurses on the unit or the phlebotomists from the lab or the techs from radiology, it makes them feel less and less safe. Even something seemingly innocent like, "Man, I can't believe how busy we are today," can make a patient wonder if they'll be forgotten.

Most of us don't realize it. When we point it out, the response is often, "I said what? Really? I don't even remember that." I'm guilty of it, myself. I was admiring a new baby in the postpartum unit and said, "Look how much hair it has. So cute!" When the person with me said, "It?" I had no idea what she was talking about. I called the newborn it? Really? I felt awful; I can't possibly know how I made the new mom feel.

Sometimes, just knowing that patients are listening intently to us is enough to help us remember to watch our words, but sometimes we need a gentle reminder. Being open to that kind of feedback will help create a safer and kinder environment for everyone.

DO YOUR COWORKERS LIKE YOU?

In the Service Excellence department, we talk a lot about how we treat patients. We do a lot of training and coaching about what patients are feeling, how best to address their needs, and how to design processes and systems that put patients at the center.

Sometimes we forget to be kind to one another, too.

There are many reasons to be kind to our colleagues: it defines the culture, it makes coming to work a whole lot better, but something else we may not realize is that patients notice. They are watching and listening to everything, and even though we may not be saying something outright negative, they know when we don't get along.

One of my favorite parts of service training is the piece about "managing up," that is, speaking well about those who precede or follow me in the patient care continuum. I like the idea of finding something nice to say about someone and making sure our patients feel like they are in the very best hands.

The other side of managing up, though, is being the kind of colleague about whom people have no problem finding something nice to say. I know for me, sometimes I get so focused on the patient experience, I can neglect the colleague experience. Am I treating my coworkers with as much consideration and courtesy? Am I the kind of person they want to work with? Am I part of the reason they like coming to work?

If I'm not, there's a very good chance the patients know it.

It makes them feel so much safer when they're in a place where people get along. They know people communicate better when they like each other. They believe people do a better job when they're working in a place they enjoy, and with people they respect.

The next time you're thinking about your patient experience efforts and training, don't forget to put a little piece in there about treating each other just as well. Your colleagues – and your patients – will appreciate it.

THE CRAFT AND CIDER PROJECT

Along with Patient Experience, part of a former role under the Service Excellence umbrella was Healing Arts. I was fortunate to be working in an organization that recognized the impact that visual arts and music has on a person's well-being and we had a number of programs for patients and their visitors.

I realized we had an opportunity to offer the same kinds of programs for our employees.

My former intern and I decided to put together an event that featured acrylic paint, small canvases and easels, a variety of brushes, non-alcoholic apple cider, and a harpist playing in the background. Employees were welcome to spend some time painting, creating, sipping apple cider and relaxing. For those who insisted they didn't know how to paint, we even hired a professional artist to come and help them tap into their inner Van Gough.

It was a hit.

We held the event in a very public space, allowing guests and visitors a chance to stop in and participate, as well. People seemed genuinely impressed that we were offering this kind of free event.

- A young woman who was visiting her husband came by looking for a way to pass the time while he slept.
- An older man with his granddaughter painted a seascape and told us he had never held a paintbrush or painted anything before. He was so grateful to be able to experience that, especially with his granddaughter.
- Two little girls visiting their grandma stopped by to paint for a while. Their parents were so thankful they had something new to do after spending so much time in our hospital.
- Several nurses and other staff members popped in on their lunch break and said they felt refreshed with renewed energy after spending 30 minutes painting with us.

A very well-received event and it didn't cost a ton of money; what more could you ask for?

If you're looking for a way to do something for your staff, consider bringing the arts to them. Even those who don't feel confident in their abilities can benefit from 30 minutes of time spent away from their department just creating. We know the impact art has on patients. It can do the same for your employees.

THOUGHTS FROM THE NIGHT SHIFT

A few years ago, I was working at a large medical center and decided to go out on the floors in an effort to connect with the night shift. As part of the leadership team I knew it was important to get out and talk with the direct-care staff, and it's especially important to visit with the often overlooked night shift.

My alarm went off at an hour when most college students are just going to bed. It was a time of night I hadn't seen in decades and I couldn't imagine how anyone could be awake, let alone work. I dragged myself into the shower hoping the steady stream of hot water would bring me back into consciousness. It worked. I got dressed, put my face on, and headed out into the dark.

When I got to the hospital, I discovered one of the few perks of working nights: plenty of parking. Plus, it's really quiet. That's something we never experience during the day.

While I was able to get through most of the hospital, I spent the majority of my time in two different med/surg units and the differences between them were startling. In the first one, the nurses seemed genuinely happy to see someone from administration. When

I walked up to them, they smiled and were very eager to talk about what they liked about working there. They had some suggestions about what could be improved but overall they were very positive. As I was leaving, I thanked them for taking time out of their very busy shift to talk to me. "No problem," they answered. "We like seeing you guys up here. Thanks for not forgetting the night nurses."

I walked toward the elevator smiling. "Wow," I thought. "This is great. This is going to be a really good night."

The other unit was completely different. I approached the small group of nurses at the desk and introduced myself. "Hi, my name's Kate. I'm the director of patient experience and I'm out tonight visiting the units to..."

"Ambush us?" said the tall one.

"Oh my goodness, no," I said. "Is that what you think?" She shrugged and said, "Well, we never see you guys here. Something must be up."

I spent the next several minutes trying to reassure her and the others that this was something the leadership team was committed to doing: getting out on the floors and talking to the people who are caring for patients, both days and nights. They seemed unconvinced.

After some gentle prodding, they opened up a bit about what it's like to work nights. The thing they liked best, they said, was the teamwork. They felt they didn't have the same resources as the day shift so they pull together and help each other out. And while they complain that they never see anyone from administration, they like that they never see anyone from administration. They said they feel more free to just be nurses without having management looking over their shoulder every minute.

That struck a nerve. Free to be nurses without management looking over their shoulder? Wow. What had we done to make them feel this way?

I asked them to tell me more about that and, essentially, it all boiled down to one thing: their manager acted more like a taskmaster than a supporter. The relationship was less about re-engaging great nurses to continue doing great work and more about pointing out all the things they were doing wrong. We do ask a lot of our direct-care staff, that's true, and for good reason: we want patients to be safe and feel well cared for. But there's a way to ensure that all of those required steps – like asking a patient's name and birthdate before giving a medication or foaming in and out of patient rooms – are done without it coming across as punitive.

Until we give our new leaders the right training on how to get the job done while still serving as an ally, a resource, a champion for the staff, we will hear things like I heard: just let us be nurses.

I DID MY JOB

Lately, I've been participating in some skills training that focuses a lot on checklists. I think there's a lot to be said for being very specific when you're trying to teach someone how to interact professionally and compassionately with people. For many, these skills don't come naturally, so we need to illustrate some concrete actions that demonstrate warmth and caring. Simply telling someone to be nice isn't very helpful. Everyone thinks they're nice.

There's no shortage of checklists out there for behavioral standards and ways to make patients feel more comfortable, but what if you do all the things on the checklist and patients are still unhappy?

I had a coaching session with someone for this very thing. He couldn't understand why, after doing everything he was taught to do, patients still complained about him. He made sure he said hello, introduced himself and his role, he explained how long the tests would take and what was going to happen. He even said thank you at the end of every patient encounter. His manager was having a very difficult time giving him some helpful feedback because he was doing everything on the checklist and still not getting very good survey scores from patients.

After spending a few moments observing him, the answer was obvious. He wasn't connecting.

I was looking at a perfectly competent employee with very good technical skills who was simply going through the motions without any sincerity. He was focused on his to-do list, there to do a job and complete a series of tasks, doing just enough to not get fired.

When we put the focus solely on ourselves and our actions, we forget that experience is a two-way street. Simply doing the items on the checklist doesn't guarantee that the other person understands what we've said or interprets those things as helpful. It takes a genuine connection, even if it's brief, to demonstrate caring to a patient.

Simply saying hello doesn't convey a warm greeting but "Say Hello" was an item on the checklist. Should we have written "Sincerely and warmly greet every person with whom you come in contact"? Well, if that's what you want, then that's what you need to write if you're going to use a checklist.

A better way is to hire people for whom this comes naturally. Warmth is tough to teach.

My coaching story does have a happy ending. This employee used to display warmth and sincerity with patients, but over time, he got jaded, bored, and burned-out. All it took was a little reminder from me and he was able to reconnect with that part of himself he'd let go dormant. For those that never had it to begin with, I wonder if you can teach it. I'd rather spend my training budget helping people with the right kind of interpersonal skills and a desire to get even better.

What kinds of criteria are you using to hire your employees? Are you hiring for fit and culture?

SHOULDN'T YOU CALL IN SICK WHEN YOU'RE SICK?

How many of you work for an organization that rewards perfect attendance?

I was at an awards ceremony at a hospital not long ago. They were giving service awards to employees who had been there for 5, 10, even 40 years. The chief nurse wanted to give a certified nurse's assistant an award for never calling in sick once after working there for 35 years. I asked her if this was really a good thing. She looked at me in disbelief. "Of course it's a good thing! She's never called in, not once, in her whole time here. That's amazing. That shows real dedication."

I just stood there in stunned silence, wondering how she and I could be so far apart on this issue.

As it happened, I was friendly with this CNA, so I asked her if she had ever been sick in those 35 years and came to work anyway. "Of course," she said. "I got sick, everybody gets sick. I just put a mask on over my face and get to work."

Is this really what we want to celebrate?

As I write this, COVID-19, or coronavirus, is everywhere. There are over 250,000 cases and nearly 11,000 deaths globally. Industry conferences are being cancelled, cruise ships are being quarantined, and stores are selling out of toilet paper and hand sanitizer all across the U.S. Do we really want to incentivize employees to come to work when they don't feel well? Especially CNAs, who assist with feeding, bathing, and toileting people who are already sick?

Sick days exist for a reason. I understand not every company has them, but this one did. Generous sick leave, in fact. Part of me thinks this is a generational thing. My parents (and even me, to some extent) grew up believing that you keep your nose to the grindstone, work hard, and tough it out. I get it.

But times are changing. Even before the coronavirus, I started to see signs in workplaces and elementary schools telling people to stay home if they didn't feel good. And now, we're socially isolating, sheltering in place, self-quarantining. And it makes good sense. Keep your germs to yourself.

The fact that this chief nurse was celebrating this CNA is incentivizing all the wrong things. I think people should take care of themselves and should be given time to rest, relax, and recover. The message she sent was the opposite of that. Maybe it's generational, maybe it's her set of values, but even after this virus passes, we need to tell our employees that their health and well-being is important to us as an organization and stop handing out perfect attendance awards.

WHAT ARE WE LEARNING FROM COVID-19?

This is my 100th blog entry. I couldn't have predicted I'd still be writing after all this time, but it turns out I have a lot to say about how to care for patients and employees.

Things have changed dramatically since COVID-19 hit and I've been thinking a lot about how to best care for staff who are showing up every day and working hard to save lives.

The name Lorna Breen has been in the news a lot lately. She was an emergency medicine physician and the medical director of the emergency department at New York-Presbyterian Hospital in Manhattan. I never met her, never even heard her name until her story hit the news a few weeks ago. But I think it's important to write about her. There is so much we as healthcare leaders can learn from her story.

According to an April 27th New York Times article, Dr. Breen had contracted the coronavirus, stayed home for just a week and a half, returned to work, was sent home, then went to stay with her family in North Carolina to recuperate. Upon arriving, she was hospitalized for exhaustion for 11 days, and once discharged, went to stay with her mom, then her sister. Two days later, Dr. Breen died by suicide.

By all accounts, Dr. Breen was a fun-loving extrovert who enjoyed skiing, salsa dancing, throwing parties, and volunteering at a home for older adults. She was well liked, well respected and was always looking out for her colleagues, making sure they had enough personal protective equipment and were doing okay.

Her family said that working in the trenches with so many patients dying from the virus changed her. She would be at the end of a 12-hour shift and stay to continue helping. With patients dying in the waiting room before they could even get into the ER, Dr. Breen had said they couldn't keep up, she couldn't go home, she had to stay and help.

When you go into a profession in healthcare, you are compelled to help. When you run in when others run away, it's normal to think that if you don't do it, it won't get done. But we have to start helping these professionals see that there's no shame in putting the oxygen mask on your own face before helping others with theirs.

I'm not going to lay blame at anyone's feet. I'll just say that we have to look out for each other and insist that people go home. Rest. Recharge. I've worked in so many environments that just don't allow for that. If someone admits they're exhausted or struggling to keep going, others turn their backs and make them feel guilty. We as leaders have to change that.

Right now, we have healthcare workers, physicians, nurses, food service workers, housekeepers, IT professionals, and patient experience teams who are feeling vulnerable, frightened, and tired. We have to reach out. We have to let them know how much they mean to us and we do that not by hanging banners that say Hero, but by spending time with them. Let them talk. Listen without interrupting. Insist they go home and not stay past the end of their shift. Create programs that nurture and support them. Give them hazard pay and additional sick days. Don't just tell them, show them how much we care.

I feel terrible that Dr. Breen took her own life. I'm hopeful that we learn from this and start creating a culture that acknowledges that physicians and nurses aren't superheroes. They're people who care. Let's care for them.

WHY EMPLOYEE ENGAGEMENT = PATIENT LOYALTY

I saw a quote last week from Simon Sinek that I thought was terrific: "No customer will ever love a company until the employees love it first." I started thinking about all the places I shop and dine, as well as all the places I've worked, and found this to be true again and again.

I remember being in a coffeehouse in Chicago and being amazed at the precision and care the barista showed in making my latte. There was a beautiful flower on the top of my coffee that was different from my friend's, different from everyone's, and I was struck at the vibe this place gave off. It was like no other coffeehouse I'd been to. It hit me – the people working here love working here.

They only have a small handful of locations around the city, but they're worth going out of your way for.

Conversely, I've been in plenty of clothing stores and have overheard employees talking to one another about how much they hate it there. The hours are too much, they hate having to re-fold the shirts again and again, the boss is a jerk (yes, they said that with customers in the store), even complaining about other customers. Those are stores I don't go back to, no matter how much I like the clothes.

So, when I've been hired to do some service excellence training for employees to improve patient experience, one of the first ways I can tell if it's got a chance at being successful is to assess the level of employee satisfaction and engagement.

All too often, I see stressed out front line staff who feel like too much is being asked of them already. People who once had a passion for patient care are now feeling overworked and under – appreciated. And they are not excited about going through service excellence training.

Your patient experience efforts, good as they may be, will simply not work if your employees don't feel valued and appreciated. When employees love the work they do, respect the people they work for, and are committed and connected to the mission of the organization, it shows.

When healthcare workers like their jobs, patients can feel it.

- At their most vulnerable and dependent on others, they feel safer with a committed staff
- When facing a difficult diagnosis, they feel more supported by empathetic listeners
- When battling a vicious disease, their spirits are lifted in a warm and friendly office
- When they have questions about medications or payment options, they're more likely to ask when the staff shows care and understanding

These are the things that create loyalty, the willingness to go out of your way or even pay a little more, because of the emotional connection you feel to a place. Change your culture, re-engage your employees and your patients will be fiercely loyal to you. Not sure how? Contact me. I can help.

SIX REASONS TO EMPOWER YOUR UNIT MANAGERS

I belong to a nation-wide email list in which Patient Experience professionals can ask questions, get advice, and share experiences. I saw a question last week that I imagine is a concern for other PX managers so I decided to respond.

This patient experience manager was in the process of reorganizing responsibilities and one of the things she wanted to change was the handling of complaints. Under the current system, when a patient or family member is unhappy, the staff calls the PX manager to talk with them. It's becoming harder and harder for her to keep up, especially with all the other responsibilities she has, so her hope was to have the unit manager or department leader handle those complaints and concerns.

I've had the opportunity to establish two different patient experience departments and both times I insisted that all staff be empowered and appropriately trained to handle complaints within their own units. Here's why:

1. Patient Experience becomes everyone's responsibility when everyone has to manage and resolve patient complaints. Patient experience isn't one person's job, it's an organization-wide culture in which everyone plays a role. Employees become much more proactive and engaged when they can't simply pick up the phone and have someone else deal with their angry patient.

2. Patients and their families don't want to be handed off to the complaint department. They know the person in that role is specially trained to say all the right things to make them feel better but they don't always believe that he or she can actually do anything about it. The main reason patients voice their complaint is to be sure the issue won't happen again to anyone else. Dealing with the supervisor of that department assures them that, at the very least, the boss is aware of the problem.

3. It's far more efficient to handle complaints at the unit level. When people are unhappy, they don't want to wait to voice their concern or do it on someone else's schedule. Empowering and training staff members in service recovery demonstrates an organization-wide commitment to patient-centeredness.

4. By handling complaints at the department or unit level, the patient experience team isn't viewed as the complaint department or a 'dumping ground' for resolving problems. That department should be spending much more time shaping policy to proactively enhance and elevate the patient experience, not simply reacting to problems after they've happened.

5. Employee morale increases when they know there are people on staff who are tracking, trending and correcting patient complaints. The patient experience team should regularly report to the whole hospital on issues that had been coming up with some consistency and the steps they took to fix them. Employees hate when they think no one is listening to them or their patients; they'll be much happier at work when they see management taking action.

6. A hospital's reputation improves and patient loyalty is strengthened when complaints are handled quickly and all employees have a service attitude. It's important to remember that you're not working in a vacuum; other hospitals are working hard at improving their own patient experience. If you're not getting better, you're getting worse.

Who handles complaints at your hospital? Does *everyone* have the tools they need?

EMPLOYEE ENGAGEMENT

A couple of years ago, I attended The Cleveland Clinic's Empathy Summit, a terrific conference about patient experience, staff burnout, and relationship-centered care. Among the many powerful presentations was one about employee engagement that stuck in my head long after my flight home.

Essentially, the speaker said that no one is more excited about their job than a new employee on their first day. They come in, full of energy, ready to get started, and eager to learn all the new things about their new role. And then a year goes by and they have their annual evaluation and we see the enthusiasm has waned. Fast forward another year or so and these same eager, excited employees are now cynical, tired, and looking for a better opportunity.

We tend to blame the employees. They've lost their passion. They've forgotten why they got into this field. They just don't seem to care. What's wrong with them?

Companies will then spend all kinds of money on things designed to re-engage the workforce: they rent out an entire amusement park for a day, they have a black-tie event at a banquet hall, they host a day at a racetrack, all kinds of things.

But the speaker at the conference said simply, "The idea shouldn't be to re-engage employees, the idea should be to not beat the engagement out of them in the first place. They come to us on their first day with more excitement and enthusiasm than ever and we're the ones that drain it out of them."

Brilliant.

So what is it exactly that we're doing to them?

#1 Micromanaging

When we hire really smart people, the worst thing we can do is look over their shoulder and tell them not just what to do but how to do it. My work style isn't necessarily the same as yours and that should be okay.

#2 Not Empowering them to Make Decisions

Nothing shuts people down faster than being reprimanded for coming up with a new idea or doing something out of the box to help a customer. When workers step outside the boundaries of their job description and are slapped on the hand for it, you've guaranteed they'll never do it again.

#3 Pigeonholing Them

One of the worst things you can do to a person is think of them only in terms of their title. When an employee expresses a desire to learn a new skill or move to a different department, we should encourage them. People are so much more than their job title; allow them to spread their wings a little and learn about other areas of the organization.

#4 Theory X Management

You've heard of the carrot and the stick, right? When a manager rules by fear, pits employees against one another, and says the workers' primary job is to make him look good, it's no wonder they thank God it's Friday. Carrots will always make for a more productive workforce, as will teamwork and a manager who understands servant leadership.

#5 Not Aligning Goals with Resources

Employees need certain tools and resources to get the job done. Asking more of them than they could possibly do and not providing the staff or equipment to get it done is a great way to frustrate and demotivate.

The next time you're at a new employee orientation, take a look around the room at all the excited new faces and ask yourself how you can keep that excitement going, instead of trying to re-engage it after it's gone.

CONTINUED EMPLOYEE ENGAGEMENT

A few months ago, I wrote a piece about employee engagement. I said that employees are never more excited to be at your organization than on the first day. Over time, as their excitement begins to wane and they become bored and even cynical, we tend to blame them rather than looking at all the ways we drained their enthusiasm from them.

Instead of frustrating and de-motivating our employees in ways we probably don't even realize, what can we do instead?

1. Periodically have your team reflect on what they enjoy about their role. When they can tell you what they like about what they do, they won't lose sight of it.

2. Remember to tell them you appreciate them. For me, it's important to mix in professional achievements in with personal attributes. I don't want to be acknowledged only when I produce for the boss. I like to be recognized for who I am, as well.

BETTER THAN I FOUND IT

3. Give them as much freedom as they can handle. Some employees, especially ones in new roles, prefer more structure and assistance. Others prefer – and do well with – less oversight. Know who's who and adjust your management style appropriately.

4. Go to bat for them. Sometimes, there are conflicts between departments that require leadership to get involved. Show your employees that you have their backs by listening to their side of the story before confronting them. If it truly was their fault, help them come up with ways to avoid the same problem in the future.

5. Encourage the team to work together. One of the worst things we can do as leaders is to create competition within the department. Showing obvious favoritism doesn't encourage staff to work harder to win your favor; it makes them resent the favorite – and you.

6. Let them know what you're up to. Many leaders keep their employees in the dark about things they're planning or changes that are coming in the company. Certainly, keep confidential and sensitive information out of bounds, but if you're working on important things that will affect the team, tell them. Keeping them in the dark only frustrates them, especially when they hear rumors they know nothing about.

7. Plan something fun. Better yet – let them plan something fun. If you're able to go off-site, give them some options and let them choose where they'd like to go and what they'd like to do. If that's not possible, bring in lunch for everyone every so often and eat with them.

8.   Keep tying the work of the department to the larger mission of the organization. When there's conflict or disagreement about how to move forward, bring them back to why we're here and what we're trying to do.

9.   Set clear expectations not only about the work but about behavior. When you hear people speaking ill of others, whether in your department or not, put a stop to it right away. Stay consistent.

10.   Recognize that motivation will wax and wane over time. Be aware of what your team members may be going through and don't overreact if someone doesn't look as cheerful today as usual. Be accessible if they want to talk and continue to recognize and appreciate them.

The most important thing to remember is that it's a lot easier to keep a team motivated than it is to try and re-motivate one that's lost its enthusiasm. So instead of being upset with employees that aren't nearly as excited as they were on their first day, try not to beat that enthusiasm out of them in the first place.

Will doing all these things keep your staff from losing their fire? I can't guarantee it, but I can guarantee that they'll enjoy working for you a lot more than if you don't.

What other things do you do to keep your team engaged?

HANDLING A COMPLAINT

Looking at the woman sitting on the other side of my desk, I felt so sorry for her. Here she was, a new manager, trying to do the right thing and feeling completely defeated. "I just don't know what else to do," she said.

I wanted to give her a hug.

The dietary staff had been getting a lot of complaints about the food: it's burnt, it's too cold, it has no flavor, it's too salty, it's not what I want, it looks disgusting, the texture feels weird, this is inedible... she couldn't win.

Hospital food has always gotten a bad rap, but lately, it seemed, there had been more complaints than usual. She was in my office asking if I would do some training with her food servers so they would be able to better handle the negative feedback.

"Of course. I'd be happy to." That's my standard answer to just about everything. But in her case, I sincerely meant it.

Not wanting to contradict anything already happening in her department, I asked her what kind of training they've had up to this point. "Not a whole lot, really. If someone says they don't like the meatballs, for example, I usually say something like, 'I love the meatballs! That's one of my favorite dishes here!'"

I stared at her for just a moment and wondered if any waiter in any fancy restaurant would ever say something like that. "You know, the patients don't really care what *you* like," I told her. "It's all about what *they* like."

She paused. "Hmmm. I guess you're right."

"Tell you what," I said, "Tell me what your biggest issues are and I'll design a training class to address them so we can give your staff some tools for handling those things."

Her face brightened. "Really? That would be wonderful!"

"Of course. I'd be happy to." I still sincerely meant it.

It got me thinking, when people complain about something, our natural instinct is to either get defensive or try to convince them they're wrong. What we should do is apologize and try to fix it. "You don't like the meatballs? Oh, I'm so sorry. What can I get for you instead?"

You'll notice I didn't say, "Is there something else I can get for you?" Open-ended questions are always better. It indicates that I *will* get something else for you; you just need to tell me what.

I started working on a training program.

- First, listen to the person. Listen to understand, not to respond. Don't interrupt. Don't argue.

- Second, apologize. Not to admit fault, but to express regret for their experience. "I'm so sorry this happened," or "I'm sorry this has been your experience."

- Third, serve the need. Do whatever you can to make it right and if you can't, find someone who can.

- Finally, thank them. "I'm so glad you brought this to my attention. We can't fix it if we don't know there's an issue. Thank you for telling me."

Okay, you may have noticed that this is not my own original model, but there's a reason why so many places use this model – it works. It isn't easy to actually do, especially when you're facing someone who is angry, shouting, or just plain mean, but it's truly the best way to shift the focus off of you and that person and focus instead on the issue.

I plan on doing a bunch of role-playing in this training. Everybody loves role-playing, right? Okay, nobody loves role-playing but it really is the best way to sharpen your skills in a less stressful environment. I asked for the top 3 complaints the team hears most often, and I'm designing scenarios around them for the group to act out. Tools for the toolbox and a bit of practice before we send them out to the real thing.

I can't guarantee they won't keep getting complaints, but at least they'll know how to better handle them.

WE ALREADY DO THIS

In the many years I've been leading service trainings across the country, I have yet to teach a class that didn't have at least one person who truly resents being there. Sometimes, those people are the ones who think what you're teaching is nonsense: all that touchy-feely stuff, that's not what I do. I do my job, I don't have to be nice about it.

I know how to handle those folks; they don't bother me. I'll gently cajole, end a lot of sentences with, "Don't you think?" or, "Right?" and try to let the members of the class be the ones to drive the message home.

It's the ones who feel they already know all this, they already do all this, and this training is a waste of time. Those ones are harder because they believe in delivering great service and I don't want to talk down to them and cause them to disengage. But with so many others in the class for whom these are new skills, I have to slow it down and make sure they understand and feel comfortable using these new skills.

So how do you teach a class full of people who believe they already know all this stuff?

1. Tell them that this is a new experience for them. The information may be things they've already heard, but this class is designed to help them see service in a new way, reinforce what they already know, and keep service top-of-mind.

2. Tell them that the training is to get everyone in the organization to perform at a certain level, a level that some of them are already achieving. I talk about how someone can do a beautiful job working with a patient or visitor and one knucklehead can undo all that great work in just one interaction. Each person's great work lasts when everyone delivers great service.

3. Tell them that many of us believe we do this all the time when we probably only do it most of the time. I always use myself in this example. I know I'm a nice person but am I *always* nice? Maybe not. Always is a high bar to clear and consistency is what separates great organizations from good ones.

4. Do some role playing. Involve everyone in the process and allow your 'star students' an opportunity to show what they know. It's especially helpful if you can give them a scenario that is outside their normal process. If they're nurses, give them a scenario that applies to IT or environmental services.

5. Involve them in the process. When I get to a new talking point, I look at them and say, "You do this all the time right? Tell me how this works in your department." Asking them to give examples of what they do demonstrates that I know they do great work and allows them to act as the expert. Now, we are teaching the class, not just me.

The goal, of course, is to not have people in the class sit there with their arms folded, resenting the fact that they had to sit through this stupid class where they already knew everything. The goal is to get everyone to engage, participate, and actually enjoy the class.

Sure, there will be some who think the whole thing is non-sense, but for those who believe in the message and try to live it everyday, do everything you can to involve them in the process and let them be your biggest champions.

...BUT I DON'T DEAL WITH PATIENTS

Early on when I first started doing Patient Experience training, I spent a lot of time talking about all the ways we can better connect with patients, starting with simple courtesy and friendliness and moving to more personalized interactions with them, like the Platinum Rule.

The nurses, medical assistants, reception and scheduling teams were always very complimentary on their evaluation forms after completing one of my sessions. But I seemed to miss the mark when it came to the non-clinical staff who didn't interact with patients. Over and over again, I saw the same comment, "Good presenter, but I don't deal with patients. This training had nothing to do with my job."

The Information Technology staff saw themselves as I.T. experts who were there to ensure that users were able to log in and everything computer-related was working. Whether they worked in an office building or a hospital didn't seem to matter; their approach to their work was identical.

Same thing with the finance team. They were brilliant when it came to budgets and forecasts and managing accounts receivable and accounts payable. But they hadn't connected the dots as to how their role impacts patient experience.

My talking about connecting to purpose and focusing on the tactical ways we connect with patients and their families didn't resonate at all with them.

So I started focusing on company culture.

My trainings began to emphasize everyone's role in creating exceptional service for everyone: patients, their families, and other employees. It wasn't just fixing a computer system, it was ensuring that the electronic medical record didn't go down right in the middle of an exam, creating a whole bunch of headaches for staff and patients alike. The 'why' behind the 'what' began to drive the content of each session.

Soon, my evaluation forms were reflecting the change and, more importantly, the patient satisfaction and employee engagement scores were improving. People in all departments started feeling like they were a part of something bigger, more important and meaningful.

When putting together new employee orientation and on-boarding, it's imperative to help every individual understand how his or her role contributes to delivering exceptional experiences at every turn. Once employees see themselves as part of the process, you won't hear "This training has nothing to do with my job," again.

SECTION FOUR:
THE "WHO YOU ARE" STORIES

A big question that comes up a lot in the patient experience space is "Can you teach empathy?"

I believe you can teach anybody anything, it'll just be more difficult with some people. I had to retake my college algebra class a few times but I still think someone out there could teach me calculus. It'll take a good long while, but if I really tried, I'm sure I could get it. One day.

I wanted to devote a whole section to who you are for a few reasons. As this field grows, we are beginning to recognize there are many approaches to improving patient experience. We used to focus only on the cosmetic stuff: gorgeous hospital lobbies, all private rooms, and valet parking. We moved to AIDET and being very prescriptive about exactly what staff are to say and how they're supposed to say it.

While we still utilize these things, we're realizing that there's a lot more room for creativity and innovation than we previously thought, and many personality types who can be equally effective. Some are the empaths who get up close and personal and do a great job with service recovery. Some are data-driven who can analyze and strategize and see the bigger processes at work. Some excel at public speaking or teaching. Some are more clinically focused.

But it really doesn't matter. If you have a desire to want to make things better in healthcare, there's room for you at this table.

I also wanted to write this chapter to get back to the power of one. Yes, there are systems and processes much bigger than each of us that can make this work more difficult. But ultimately, it comes down to who we're bringing in to work each day. We've all had our share of bad days and there are plenty of times I would have loved to scream in someone's face. But I don't. My one bad action will cause a ripple effect I can't even imagine. And as good as it might feel in that moment, it will feel horrible as those ripples continue.

So with personal accountability and individual creativity as the backdrop, I hope you enjoy the Who You Are stories.

THE ART LESSON

A few years ago, my department planned one of those bonding events in which employees are supposed to get together as a team outside of work hours and do something fun. Admittedly, I had my doubts about just how much *fun* it was going to be, but, in retrospect, I'm really glad I went.

We all gathered at a local place where a professional had painted a beautiful picture and we each had an easel, some paint and a brush and, most importantly, wine.

There were a few in my group who were really quite good painters. They were incredibly focused on the task at hand and tried to make their painting as close to the original as they could, right down to the number of snowflakes and the exact placement of each.

I took a different approach.

I liked the picture the artist had painted but I didn't want to create one that looked just like it. I remembered something I had told my daughter years earlier when we were at the Art Institute of Chicago. She was probably in second grade and asked me about a painting that was confusing to her. "Don't ask what it is," I told her. "Ask how it makes you feel."

I tapped into something deep inside and painted how the picture made me feel. It was a suggestion of the original, but with different colors and a different energy. It was my version of the artist's work.

At the end of the night, we all posed for a photo, each of us holding our works of art. Everyone in my group was holding a painting that looked very much like the original. Mine was decidedly different. And I was never more proud.

Okay, what does this have to do with patient experience?

It has everything to do with finding *your* voice in your approach to work. This is still an emerging field and, while there are many best practices out there that we can learn from, there is still plenty of room for innovation, creativity, and thinking differently about how to get to the heart of patient engagement.

In short, you don't have to simply do what others are doing. You can be inspired by the work that's being done and then tap into something inside of you and create something new. Test it, try it out, but never stop looking inside of you for answers. If there's a voice in your head that's telling you there's a better way, listen to it! Design a pilot program around it and try it out.

There's a reason you went into this field. You're passionate about it. You know more than you think you do. Don't be satisfied to simply copy and paste. Network. Discuss. Share. Create. Innovate. Do how it makes you feel.

CHANGE HAPPENS TOGETHER

As I'm writing this, I've just left the 2018 Beryl Institute Patient Experience Conference in my hometown of Chicago. It was great to be back in the Windy City to attend the conference, catch up with old friends, and enjoy some of that tasty food I dearly miss.

Moving 2000 miles across the country to beautiful Lake Tahoe two years ago was quite a change and it took me a little while before I felt connected there. These past few days in Chicago, at this fabulous conference, reminded me how important connection is.

Jason Wolf, the President of the Beryl Institute, opened the conference by telling us that we are all part of a movement. We are a group of people working together to advance our shared ideas. And we can only get things done together, not in a room alone with just ourselves and an idea.

It made me realize – that's what I had been doing when I first arrived in Tahoe. I'd been sitting alone in front of my computer writing about patient experience, employee engagement, and hospital culture at iamthepatientexperience.net. And while that's nice, it's not enough. I felt much more energized when I joined the Service Excellence team at the big hospital here.

When nearly 1200 people came together in the Grand Ballroom of the Hyatt Regency, we could feel the power we had. 1200 people from all over the country who believed in the power of human kindness and connectedness, who believed that change is possible. This is what we do, who we are. It felt amazing.

I hosted a breakfast roundtable discussion one morning about forming an effective Patient and Family Advisory Council and was so delighted with the people who came and the things they said. It felt amazing.

The next morning, I sat in on another breakfast roundtable discussion about sustaining culture and was so inspired by the ideas being discussed. The level of dedication these professionals had, ensuring they were delivering on service every single time was impressive. It felt amazing.

In each of the general sessions and smaller breakout sessions I attended, there was a feeling of togetherness, that we were all rowing the boat in the same direction. No nay-sayers, no skeptics, no one trying to poke holes in the data or tell you they've tried that before and it didn't work. Just a group of people working together to advance our shared ideas. It felt amazing.

Don't get me wrong, I like sitting alone in front of my computer, writing about the patient experience. It feels good, but it doesn't feel amazing.

Connection is what will make the patient experience dream a reality. It starts with bringing back that enthusiasm to my colleagues out west and keeping the passion alive. Getting involved in organizations like the Beryl Institute, joining more committees, sitting on more boards, reaching out to community partners. THAT is what will continue to drive this movement. It feels amazing.

POSITIVE THOUGHTS ON POSITIVITY

Earlier this morning as I was doing my daily patient rounding, one of the nurses I'd said 'good morning' to smiled and told me how much she enjoyed seeing me every day. "You always have such a positive energy around you," she said. "It really brings the mood up when you come and talk to patients and to us. I really appreciate you."

Wow. What a lovely thing to hear.

I sort of blushed and said thank you but what I really wanted to tell her was that it was a very deliberate decision every morning to show up with a smile.

We patient experience directors have to walk a tricky line. On the one hand, we're trying to dispel the outdated thinking that patient experience is 'fluff stuff' led by a bunch of vapid do-gooders who have no clue about real life. And at the same time, we can't appear jaded and cynical or give in to all the forces that tell us that other things are more important.

I've taken a bit of heat in my career trying to be positive. I've encountered plenty of eye rolls, arms folded firmly across chests, sarcasm, and open hostility. I've been dismissed from meetings with a flick of the wrist, interrupted, had my data challenged in every conceivable way, and told 'that's nice, but we have real work to do.'

I've even had patients tell me to leave when I've come to round on them after learning I wasn't a physician or a nurse. If I can't give them pain meds then what good am I?

I have to choose to be positive. But honestly, why would I choose to be anything else?

I've been angry, frustrated, outspoken, sarcastic, and cynical myself and you know where it got me? No further than being positive. Being positive just makes me feel better. Noticing the good, recognizing when something goes well, celebrating people who give a little extra... these things make me happy. And knowing that by doing them I can make someone else happy makes me even more happy.

Staff perform better when the culture is positive. The world has enough desk pounders, enough cynics, enough people who are eager to rain on your parade. If I expect staff to be supportive and friendly and caring to patients, how can I not be that way to them?

So yes, when I walk in the front door, step off the elevator, and onto a med/surg unit, I am smiling. I am positive. Even if I have to fake it for a few minutes. Fluff stuff? No way. I'm changing healthcare.

LEAN INTO CONFLICT

I hate conflict.

I'm all about harmony and everybody getting along. I know the world generally doesn't work like that, but I wish it did. It makes me so uncomfortable when there's tension between people.

Years ago, when I was working in organ donation and transplant, my job was to go in and speak to people who had just suffered a loss and ask them if they'd be willing to donate their loved one's organs. As you might imagine, not everyone was receptive.

One case in particular that stands out in my memory was of a young girl, around 17, who had fallen off the back of a moving car. She'd suffered a pretty bad head injury but had started to make a recovery. However, a day or so before she was to be transferred to rehab, she suffered a respiratory arrest and was declared brain dead. Her parents were devastated.

The hospital staff gave our organization a call and when I arrived I was warned by the nurses that the father was really angry. (Well, yeah, that's pretty much what I expected). They led me into a room to talk to the parents and wished me good luck while they rolled their eyes.

To no one's surprise, the father was very upset, difficult to talk to, and not terribly interested in talking about how this tragedy could turn into something positive for another family. After some period of time, however, he began to talk to me about his daughter, how beautiful and smart she was, and how he couldn't imagine their lives without her.

He and his wife eventually made the decision to donate but not because of anything I said. I just spent some time listening. As difficult as it was to go into that room knowing I had an angry dad waiting for me, I did it. I sat with him. I listened to him. I didn't try to fix it or say anything to make it better. I was just there.

I saw the same things while I was working in an acute care hospital. Patients or their family members would be really upset about what's happening and instead of moving toward the complaint, so many staff members would move away, avoid, focus on quieting them down instead of hearing them.

Again and again they'd say things like, "Don't go in there, he's really angry." While I understand that it's difficult to deal with an angry person, they're exactly the people we need to be dealing with. If they can verbalize their frustration, if they can tell us what the problem is, then we have a chance of fixing it. And even if we can't, we will have made their experience a little better just by having heard them.

I still hate conflict, but I'm choosing to see it as a chance to make a bad situation a little better. How about you?

TWO EYES, TWO EARS, ONE MOUTH

I think we're wired to want to fix things, to try to make things better. Certain professions in particular are all about fixing things: mechanic, plumber, physician, to name a few. It's great to be a fixer. You can take something that's broken and make it work again, you have skills that others don't have, you can do things that others can't. We all want to feel like we have some special ability to fix something and make it better.

What's difficult sometimes, is knowing when to step in and fix and when to hold back and support. Parents are faced with this all the time; it's easier to just tie your kid's shoelaces every morning, but at some point, you have to let her do it herself. Spouses, too, are faced with this when their partner comes home from work and wants to vent. It's tempting to jump in with a solution to the problem, but that's usually not what the other wants.

When you work in Patient Experience, especially if you're a Certified Patient Experience Professional (CPXP) you're the subject matter expert. You've done your homework, you know what works, and you've probably seen your share of failed attempts so you know what *not* to do. The thing is, you're not supposed to be a fixer. Your role is to work collaboratively with the team, not to come in and take over.

That can be a really difficult role. You're being paid for your expertise, but, unlike a mechanic or a plumber, patient experience is a team sport. Many people have to participate in order for the improvement efforts to work. Coming in and taking over isn't the way to get people on board.

When I was little, my mom used to tell me that I had two eyes, two ears and one mouth for a reason: before you speak, look around and listen. Pay attention to what's going on around you and really listen to what others are saying before you start talking. That's easier said than done most times, but it's a good reminder that sometimes it's best to wait.

When you need to enlist the support and participation of a group, remember: two eyes, two ears, one mouth.

WHAT'S YOUR APPROACH TO PROBLEMS?

One of the cool things I got to do within a former health system was co-facilitate half-day retreats focused on kindness and empathy. These retreats are designed to reiterate the organization's values with staff after they've been with us for 3 or 4 months. We talked about ways they've seen these values play out along with ways they, themselves, could make their hospitals better places to work.

One of the exercises explores communication styles and how we deal with patient complaints. We boiled it down to 4 main types:

- **The how**: these people are process-driven and want to understand how things unfolded as they did and how we can make changes so they don't happen that way again.

- **The why**: these are the visionaries. They are future-focused and imagine the possibilities of designing a system that supports the people and the process.

- **The who**: the people-people. Their main concern is taking care of people's feelings. They can't change what happened so they focus on caring for the people involved.

- **The what**: these folks take action. They'll make a list of the issues, rank them in order of importance and get busy fixing them..

As a facilitator, I was supposed to remain dispassionate and espouse the virtues of each group, but it's plain to see that I'm a 'who' person. I am fully invested in the people and how they feel. It's not better or worse than any other group, but it's clearly me.

I'd spend a few moments with each group, helping them through the exercise and facilitating the discussion. The group I always found most interesting was the 'what' group. These are the action-oriented people who want to get to the business of fixing things as quickly as possible.

They acknowledged they can be seen as cold by the 'who' people but they felt they were the most helpful; they're going to fix the problem. And isn't that why people complain in the first place, to get things fixed? As one class said, it's not a therapy session, it's a grievance.

After listening to that group explain their motives, I finally understood why some families would roll their eyes at me when I said things like, "I can't imagine how difficult this must have been for you," or "I see your frustration, I'm sure I'd feel the same way if this had happened to me." They aren't about the feelings. They want it fixed.

I get it.

And that's the real point of the exercise: we are all different in how we approach problems, so we all need to work together to fix them. We can often miss things when we work alone but working together gives us a more complete solution.

This part of the retreat was often the most highly-rated section. It helped the participants appreciate other people's communication styles and understand the limits of their own. And it was a nice example of teamwork and being part of something bigger than yourself. I'm so glad I got to be a part of it and see the fixers in a whole new way.

THE APPROACHES IN ACTION

Last time, I wrote about the company retreat I helped facilitate that focused on empathy, kindness and communication styles. As a person who is very focused on caring for people, I was interested to talk with those who focus on the action of fixing the problem, not so much the feelings of the people involved.

Timing is everything. Just a few days later, I received a phone call from one of our hospitalist physicians asking for my help. There was a patient on our med/surg unit who was very unhappy. This physician had done his best to make things better, but the patient really wanted to complain to someone in administration. And so, I was on my way.

I got off the elevator and made my way to the nurses' station where he was waiting for me, and along with him was the director of the unit. He had been telling her about this unhappy patient and when I said I was going in to speak with him, she offered to come, too.

"Let's do this together," she said. "I don't do the touchy-feely stuff, that's not really what I'm good at." "Sometimes, that's not what's needed," I answered, remembering what we had covered in that retreat the week before. "Maybe he's not a touchy-feely type. Let's see what he says."

We entered his room and introduced ourselves. He proceeded to tell us all about the things he was unhappy with. We listened intently. Everything he complained about, she wrote down and when he was finished, she immediately sprang into action. She told him all the things she was going to do and how long she'd be gone and then went off to get started. I stayed behind.

He told me how much he appreciated people like her. It was clear that she cared and was going to do everything she could to fix the issues, but to him, what was done was done and no amount of fixing was going to change that.

Rather than feel powerless, I decided to go after the touchy-feely. I'd noticed a Happy Birthday balloon in the corner of the room and asked if it was his birthday. "Yesterday. My daughter brought me that."

"You had to celebrate your birthday in the hospital? I'm so sorry to hear that. That's not a fun way to spend your birthday!"

"Yeah, well I don't know how many more I'm going to have so I'm happy to spend them anywhere," he said. The tone of the room changed and his face went from serious to sad. "I don't mean to be one of those patients who complains about everything," he said. "I just want people to care, to do a good job, to deliver what they promise. You have people here who just don't seem to care. This director, she cares. You can tell that things matter to her. Look, she solved my problem in two seconds. But others... they're just sleepwalking."

I told him how sorry I was that this was how he had experienced us. "That's not who we are," I said. "That's not how we want you to think of us." He reached for my hand. "Thank you. I know you two are doing your best." He sort of half smiled and closed his eyes.

At that point, the director came back in and told him what she had done to fix his complaint. He thanked her, smiled at me, and closed his eyes again.

The two of us walked back to the elevator, happy that she was able to address the action items and I was able to address the touchy-feely part.

The whole time, I kept thinking about what I'd experienced in that retreat and how important it is to work with people who fill in your holes, people who can do the things that you can't. Instead of seeing another's strengths as better than or inferior to yours, think of them as complementary to yours. Instead of competing, try collaborating.

It's probably the best thing you can do for your patients.

WHEN IT'S GOOD TO
BE SENSITIVE

Ever since I was a little kid, I remember my parents telling me I was too sensitive. When I was in 2nd grade, my Brownie troop took a trip to the movies where we saw "For The Love of Benji." For those of you unfamiliar, Benji, the family dog, gets lost when they all take a trip to Greece and they spend the whole movie trying to find him.

I cried and cried. Poor Benji, he's lost in a foreign country and can't find his way back to his family... it was more than my 7-year-old heart could take. The Brownie troop leader had to take me out to the lobby and sit with me until I could pull myself together. The other Brownies had no idea why I was so upset.

My tender heart got a little tougher as I got older but I still find myself being the only one in my family moved to tears at a rescue shelter, a Broadway show, or even a home-for-the-holidays-themed commercial. In the family reunion of my stoic, stiff upper lip northern European relatives, I'm a sensitive soul.

I've learned, though, that sensitive doesn't just mean *cries at the drop of a hat.* Sensitive also means I pick up on things that others often miss, and it has served me well in this line of work.

When I'm talking with an upset family, I scan the room and notice everything. From the personal belongings in the patient room to the amount of eye contact the family members make with one another, I take it all in and use it to help me better understand and connect with them. Even with my colleagues, I'm usually the first to notice when someone is not quite themselves and I'm quick to change my communication style to suit the tone of the meeting. I'm sensitive. I notice.

Not everyone does. There have been plenty of meetings after which I left feeling emotionally drained while everyone else was just fine, unaffected, oblivious to the tension in the room.

True, it's not always easy. It's hard to be in tune with how other people feel and then take on those feelings, myself. But if I'm going to convey kindness, compassion, and empathy in my work, I need to. It seems only natural. If I can't understand why they're so upset, how can I be moved to action to make it better? So many people will listen to a complaint, say all the right things, promise to make some improvements, then simply walk away and do nothing more. When you feel what they feel and understand how important it is, you do something.

Sensitive, to me, doesn't mean touchy, emotional, or weepy. It means I see things that some other people don't. I pick up on things that others may not notice. I feel things more deeply than others. I've found it valuable in patient experience work. Not so much at a Benji movie.

CELEBRATE YOUR GIFTS

I've recently become aware that I celebrate other people's skills more than my own. It's a lot easier for me to tell you about my friends' talents, skills, and abilities. I can brag all day about how amazing they are. I have a friend who can sit at a piano and play beautifully, anytime. No sheet music, no chord charts required. It always makes me smile.

Another friend has the gift of being able to make friends anywhere she goes. She isn't afraid to talk to anyone, and always has tons of people around her. Another is incredibly handy around the house. She can fix just about anything.

They're all very different but I admire them all equally. They can do things I can't.

To me, my talents don't seem like any big deal. I assume that if I can do it, anyone can. After all, I'm nobody special, am I? Well, special or not, I have unique personal and professional experiences that make me valuable.

I got into a conversation with a co-worker about previous jobs and when I told her I had interned at a counseling center for victims of domestic violence, worked at a rape crisis center, and had spent many years asking the families of recently deceased patients if they would donate their loved one's organs, her response surprised me.

"Oh my goodness, you did that? Really? How could you do that?"

My answer was, "Somebody has to."

And then I realized that not everyone can.

It's important to identify and appreciate the gifts you've been given. You don't have to be the best at something in order for it to be important and valuable. You have to bring the uniqueness of you to it. Sometimes, there's something about you that inspires, affects, touches, or impacts a person or process like no one else could. That's your gift.

What does this have to do with patient experience or corporate culture?

When people assume that someone else can do it better or think it is someone else's area of expertise, they stop recognizing their own unique gifts. The experts in the field can and should always be learning from others. Even at the trainings I facilitate, I ask participants what they would do in certain situations and I'm often very impressed with some of the service recovery ideas they come up with. They wouldn't consider themselves experts. They didn't think that what they did was any big deal, but to me and to others, it was amazing.

Take a few moments to see yourself through the eyes of your best friends. Celebrate what they love about you. Don't be afraid to speak up at work and make a difference. Realize that there is only one you. That's your superpower.

WHOSE GIFTS ARE 'BETTER'?

I admit, I'm in awe of people who can do complex math problems in their heads. Okay, truthfully, I'm in awe of people who can do pretty much any math problem in their heads.

But spending my time being envious of people for the skills they have, especially ones that I lack, makes me de-value my own skills and abilities.

I like to think that we were created differently so that we would find people with different gifts and achieve together what we could never do on our own.

My sister used to feel that asking for help was a sign of weakness; that everyone should be able to take care of things for themselves. Admitting she couldn't do something just wasn't an option for her. But, really, how ridiculous is that? Not everyone could possibly do everything. Even the most skilled plumber has to find a good electrician in order to build a house.

I've tried to become well-rounded and learn a bunch of different things, but at the end of the day, I know what my strengths are. They don't include math but they're important, valuable, and not everyone else has them.

I think it's easy to get sucked into the 'my skills are better than yours' way of thinking because of how we pay people. Teachers, nurses, social workers, even primary care physicians, are typically paid less than accountants, lawyers, neurosurgeons, but they're no less important, are they?

If you find yourself envying people for the things they can do that you can't, remember they are likely envious of you for something you can do. Everyone's gifts matter. Celebrate the differences. Use your talents to the very best of your ability. Connect with people who have different skills than you and watch in amazement what you can accomplish when you work together.

DO YOU NEED TO BE
A NURSE?

"Are you a nurse?" It's a question I get asked a lot, mostly by nurses, and I wonder sometimes if it would have made a difference in my career.

When it comes to patient experience, the service trainings and other improvement efforts we spearhead are geared primarily toward nurses. Nurses comprise the largest percentage of the workforce in hospitals and they are typically the ones patients remember, even more than physicians. Of course we have training for ancillary staff and non-clinical teams but most of our conversations about patient experience involve nurses.

I'm sure if I had RN after my name it would change my perspective. I'd be a lot more comfortable on the floors, going in and out of patient rooms, and knowing what to do in case of a medical emergency. I'd have a much better understanding of what it's like to work on a med-surg floor, trying to manage the many demands of patients, their families, and physicians, not to mention entering everything into the electronic medical record and the countless other things nurses have to do for 8-12 hours straight.

Am I really qualified to tell them how to deliver better care and service?

You might think not, but more and more, the people we're hearing from in the patient experience conversation these days are the patients, themselves. We read their comments from the surveys and bring them in to tell their stories of what it was like when they were lying helpless in a hospital bed.

Many keynote speakers at Patient Experience conferences are not nurses, but patients. They're people who talk about how frightened they were and how much they needed the hospital staff to show them some compassion and kindness. Patient and Family Advisory Councils and Focus Groups are widely used to suggest changes and improvements to the way care is delivered. And you know what? Nurses listen.

So I ask the question: do you need to be a nurse to be a good patient experience leader?

My opinion, of course, is no. While being an RN would give me a different perspective, it wouldn't necessarily give me a better one. When you're a hammer, everything tends to look like a nail and patient experience is more than nursing care.

I work with physicians, housekeepers, billers and coders, security guards, registrars, telephone operators, and many others, all of whom are involved in patient experience efforts. While I need to understand their perspective, I don't need to have lived it, myself. I've never been a server in a restaurant but I know good service from bad.

I think what's at the root of the question, "Are you a nurse?" is that nurses want to know that we understand how difficult their job can be. I think they're worried that some administrative pencil pusher is going to try to tell them how to do their job.

That's not my style.

I think what makes for a good patient experience professional has less to do with the initials after your name and more to do with the love inside your heart.

- Can you stay calm when people are yelling?
- Can you listen to criticism without getting defensive?
- Can you de-escalate a tense situation?
- Can you resolve a problem without throwing another person or department under the bus?
- Can you inspire people to action around a common goal?
- Can you figure out a way to present dry, dull data in an engaging way?
- Can you genuinely connect with another person, especially one in some kind of pain, and convey sincere kindness and caring?

I believe that's what makes for a good patient experience professional, nurse or not.

FOR THE NON-CLINICAL PATIENT EXPERIENCE LEADER

Last time, I asked the question: "Do you have to be a nurse to be a good patient experience professional?"

I know a lot of great patient experience leaders who are nurses but I don't think an RN is a prerequisite. Sure, being a nurse gives you some street cred when you first walk onto a unit and nurses might be a little more inclined to listen to you because they know you know what their job is like. But it's not everything.

So what should we non-clinical patient experience leaders do?

1. Listen to and support the clinical staff. This is the most important part of the job. Nurses that feel respected deliver better patient care.

2. Never immediately assume that the patient is telling you the whole story. The patient is telling you the story as he sees it. ALWAYS get the story from the nurse, too.

3. Remove ridiculous and repetitive work. As an administrator, you have the power to make things easier for nurses.

Ask them to tell you what makes their work difficult and then do everything you can to get rid of those things.

4. Recognize and reward. Tell them, show them, do whatever you need to do to demonstrate how much you appreciate them.

5. Hold them accountable for bad behavior. Let's be honest, every now and again people are going to say or do something they shouldn't but make your expectations clear and hold them to that standard. We should never meet rudeness with rudeness.

6. Keep what's best for the patient as your "True North" when faced with a difficult decision. It's not about making them happy, it's about doing what's best for them.

7. Spend some time on the floors shadowing a nurse. If you really want to know what it's like, schedule a few hours out there with them. Don't judge, don't evaluate, just stay with them. It's an eye-opener.

8. Talk to clinical staff as partners, not subordinates. After all, you can't do the work yourself. All of those ideas you have about improving things for patients, they are the ones that are going to be carrying those out. Talk *with* them, not *at* them.

9. Recognize the science behind good service. Positive patient experience is in fact tied to better clinical outcomes. Be sure your clinical staff understands that.

10. Keep learning. Consider getting certified. The exam for the CPXP designation isn't easy. Demonstrate your commitment by continuing to keep up with the research.

A good patient experience leader can't be a pollyanna, always spreading sunshine and roses (although those don't hurt). We have to have in-depth knowledge about what drives improvement. We have to know how to inspire, how to engage hearts and minds, and how to stay positive through difficult times; all things you can do with or without a nursing degree.

IS THE GLASS HALF-FULL, PART ONE

I've seen a few articles recently about the things hospitals and physician offices are doing in an effort to raise their patient experience scores. Valet parking and full service espresso bars are popping up everywhere. Nice features, to be sure, but is that really what we're talking about? What if we work in an older building that isn't so pretty? Are we doomed?

We've all heard the bit about seeing the glass half-full as opposed to half-empty, right? It's supposed to give us some insight as to whether we are optimists or pessimists, whether we choose to see things in life as possibilities or problems.

What if I told you there was another option? What if instead of trying to decide if the glass was half full or half empty, we instead looked around to find someone who might be thirsty?

This is how I choose to see things in life. It's not about optimism or pessimism; it's about seeing what's available and finding someone who needs it. It's about helping. It's about looking outside ourselves and sharing an act of kindness with another.

This kind of approach to life led me to a career in the 'softer' side of healthcare. It's not the glass of water, itself, that should be the focus. It's what we do with that glass of water that matters. If we are in a position to share that water with someone who needs it, we should. It doesn't matter if it's only half a glass. A thirsty person will appreciate it.

The patient experience movement isn't about perfection and prettiness, it's about connection. Physicians, nurses, medical techs, call center workers, front desk receptionists, etc. all have rough days, days they feel they just don't have enough gas in the tank to make a patient's experience perfect. They're tired, they're stressed, they've just been yelled at by the last patient.

But taking just a moment or two to connect, to really listen, find a way to ease a little bit of suffering… that's what the patient experience movement is about. The harpist in the lobby, the gorgeous waterfall feature, the perfectly appointed private room… those are all nice, but they're not what makes the biggest impression on patients. Patients want to be heard, cared for, listened to.

I used to work in a hospital that was in desperate need of a make-over. It was surrounded by other hospitals that were absolutely gorgeous. But people drove miles out of their way, past those fancy lobbies and tuxedoed food service workers to come to our hospital where they were treated with kindness, compassion and dignity.

Our glass was definitely half empty. We didn't look nearly as pretty as they did. But we took our half empty glass and offered it to those who needed it.

Recognize that what you have, even if it isn't perfect, may be exactly what someone else is thirsty for. Don't worry if it isn't filled to the top. The act of kindness in sharing it with someone is what matters.

IS THE GLASS HALF-FULL, PART TWO

Previously, I've written about the glass being half empty or half full and how that's supposed to be a statement about optimism or pessimism. I think what's more important is taking that glass and offering it to someone who may be thirsty.

This time, I'd like to talk about that half full (or half empty) glass and how heavy it might be.

A typical glass of water is 8 ounces, so, logically, half full is a meager 4 ounces. Very light, right?

Imagine, however, that instead of water in that glass, you have a pet peeve, an annoyance or a grudge you're holding against someone and I asked you to hold the glass up above your head. You could probably hold it up for a few minutes without any problem but after some time it would start to hurt. Hold it up for too long and you could do some serious damage to your arm.

I used to be a person who allowed myself to get easily annoyed by other people. The sound of someone crunching their food, slurping their drink, cracking their knuckles, tapping their pen, coughing, and then unwrapping a cough drop from a crinkly wrapper... oh my goodness. Drove me up a tree.

And then, I let it go. I decided that whatever annoying habit they had was too stupid to rob me of my happiness.

What does any of this have to do with patient experience?

Happy patients are, for the most part, a result of happy employees. If we are so busy fighting with each other, rolling our eyes at one another, back-stabbing or holding grudges, we are in no position to share a little kindness with our patients.

If what your co-worker is doing is truly affecting your work, you owe it to yourself and your patients to address it head on. It's uncomfortable but no one should have to be bullied at work. If your manager sides with the bully, then clearly this isn't the place for you.

But if it's nothing more serious than a pet peeve or hurt feelings from a misunderstanding, my advice to you is to put the glass down. It's only hurting your arm, not theirs. Make a decision to put down the glass before it really starts to hurt you. Choose to not let little things get under your skin. It'll take practice but it can be done.

You were called to a career in healthcare to relieve suffering. Start with your own.

THE VIRUS

One of my very best friends says, "Hardship doesn't develop character, it reveals it." I"ve never really agreed with him on that. Until recently.

At this writing, COVID-19 has changed nearly everything in our world. We cannot leave our homes unless it's to get essential supplies like food and medicine. Family members can't drop in for Sunday dinner. Seniors in retirement centers aren't allowed visitors. School is cancelled. And most people are working from home.

Healthcare workers, on the other hand, are showing up every day to care for the sick and putting their own lives at risk to do so. There is a lot of concern about capacity, staffing, and equipment like ventilators, masks, and gloves. At a time when most people are hoarding all the hand sanitizer and toilet paper, healthcare workers are walking onto the front line, risking exposure, and caring for those who need them.

In hospitals all over the United States, there is a sense of unity and teamwork. Employees are reaching out across departments to offer help where it is needed most. No longer is anything "not my job".

Even the non-clinical staff are finding ways to help. Many have created Relaxation Rooms in which staff can take a quick 10 minute break for some healthy snacks, low lighting, and calming music to recenter and recharge in order to keep going in the middle of a long shift. It's inspiring.

A close friend and former colleague who is a Director of Risk and Patient Safety said, "I'm observing improvement in communication and teamwork that I hope holds after the pandemic is over." And that's the question, isn't it: will it last? I've seen the people of this country pull together many times, be it after a hurricane like Katrina, a mass shooting like Las Vegas, and especially after 9/11. We were one nation coming together, helping one another.

Do we forget about kindness and selflessness when times are good? Do we only check in on our loved ones when we're fearful? Volunteerism shouldn't just happen in the face of tragedy. That little old lady at the end of the block could use our help grocery shopping even when there isn't a deadly virus out there.

We still have a long way to go before this is over. We have many more weeks of sheltering in place and staying home ahead of us. But once that's over, I'm hoping we still remember to call our family members and tell them we love them, visit our grandparents in the retirement center, or offer to run to the store for those who have trouble doing so. In short, **put service before self.**

If hardship really did develop character and not reveal it, it shouldn't take a pandemic to bring that out in us.

AN ATTITUDE OF GRATITUDE
WITH YOUR COWORKERS

Something I've been reading a lot about lately is gratitude. Maybe the universe is trying to send me a message, because everywhere I look, I'm seeing something about having an attitude of gratitude.

I used to think gratitude was about being thankful for what you have. It is, of course, but I've come to think of it as much more. Instead of merely looking at it from a material possessions perspective, I'm starting to be grateful for all kinds of other things.

I'm grateful for the busy days when there are a million things to do; those days fly by quickly and before I know it, it's time to go home. I'm grateful for the slow days when there isn't a lot happening; I can get caught up on the things I'd been meaning to do but never had the time.

I'm grateful for the coworker who is supportive and upbeat; she makes me feel like I'm not alone in my work. I'm grateful for the coworker who is difficult and moody; she is teaching me how to be patient and she's making me examine my own behavior and its impact on those around me.

I'm grateful for the patient who truly appreciates the work I do; he makes me feel like what I'm doing really makes a difference. I'm grateful for the patient who appears to be impossible to satisfy; he makes me step up my game, look harder for solutions, and not get complacent.

What I'm finding is that I used to only be grateful when things were going my way, but *anyone* can be grateful under happy circumstances. It's the people who can be grateful under trying circumstances, difficult circumstances, even miserable circumstances – they're the ones that truly inspire those around them.

That's the kind of coworker I want around me. That's the kind of coworker I want to be.

The next time things at work get a little tough, ask yourself how you can turn it into something to be grateful for. You might be surprised at the impact it has.

DON'T LET YOUR MOOD DICTATE YOUR MANNERS

Most of the nation is still cooped up in the house, working out of their living rooms and holding the majority of their meetings through Zoom. It's been two and a half months. We're getting restless. We're getting anxious. And we're getting a little cranky.

Until recently, I'd been living apart from my husband and daughter, working in California while they stayed behind at our home in Northern Nevada. It was a 2-3 hour drive, depending on traffic, so I rented a place near the hospital and came home on the weekends. As hard as it was being away from them, it definitely had its advantages.

It was quiet when I got home. The place was just as clean as I'd left it that morning. There was no discussion about what to have for dinner or what to watch on TV. No thermostat wars. No sharing of closet space. How much we talked to each other depended entirely on the length of our phone calls.

But I actually did miss my family. When my engagement with that hospital ended, it was nice to be back home. I really enjoyed things like having dinners together every night and not having to cram all the family time into the weekends.

And then came COVID.

No one is leaving the house. After 14 months of living apart, we are on top of each other. All day. Every day. We love each other, but we're starting to get a little tired of each other. And I'm reminded of something I learned early in my career: don't let your mood dictate your manners.

I was a new manager, trying to build a department from nothing, and working for a very demanding boss. I was having a particularly stressful day when someone I worked closely with asked me what I thought was a really obvious question and I just snapped. I don't remember exactly what I said, but it wasn't kind and the instant I said it, I wanted to take it back. I apologized, of course, but you can't take back the words you've said. Once they leave your lips, they're not yours anymore.

When we work in healthcare, or any industry in which you have to serve people, but especially healthcare when people are at their most frightened and vulnerable, we absolutely cannot let our mood dictate our manners. Whatever bad day we're having, whatever argument we had with our spouse before we left the house, whatever personal issue is going on, we can't bring it to work with us.

And even while we're at work, whatever conflict is happening with another co-worker, whatever policy is driving you crazy, none of it matters when you're with a patient or guest.

It's difficult to keep our mood in check, especially now with the additional stress of so many very sick patients and the families who are upset they can't be there with them. We're short on masks, we're worried about space and ventilators and getting sick, ourselves, or bringing this virus home to our own families. It's easy to let our mood take over and snap at the people around us.

But we can't.

We have to remember that *they're not the ones we're mad at*. If we take a moment to breathe, name the thing that's actually upsetting us, and remind ourselves that this person in front of us needs our help, we stand a better chance of continuing to be kind instead of saying something we'll regret later.

It's a good thing to remember, even after this pandemic is behind us.

SECTION FIVE:
THE PATIENT STORIES

This was a fun section to write. Lots of great memories and colorful characters.

It's funny to me that the patient section is nearly the last section in a book about patient experience. You'd think that would be the beginning but I guess the lesson here is that there's a lot of behind-the-scenes pre work that goes into a successful patient experience program.

After rereading this section, I realized that so many of the patient stories are about us, the caregivers. I'd love to make it all about them but the thing is, no matter what kinds of patients I see, the common denominator is me. I bring myself into the room every time. My perceptions, reactions, and the words I choose are all about me, not them.

Most physicians and nurses tell me that the complaints that they get are only from patients who are difficult. If the patients are reasonable, rational people, they do a great job and patients don't complain. But I measure someone's humanity by how they treat the difficult ones. Give me the tough ones and I promise you nine out of ten times I will turn them around.

Even when I was working in physician relations, I would seek out the most cranky, the most disgruntled, the most vocal and make it my mission to be their best friend within six months. It's amazing what a little kindness and some active listening can do.

So ultimately the patient stories are about us. How are we showing up to work? How do we show kindness to people who don't appear to be very kind? How do we choose to see them? That's really what it's all about. Are we bringing our best selves to every patient we meet?

REWRITE THE STORY ABOUT YOUR PATIENT

We're storytellers. With every human interaction, we're telling a story about what we see and hear. Depending on the narrative that we create in our heads, the actions of others can be completely benign or super-annoying.

Consider the patient who arrives late to an appointment. Do you immediately assume he is inconsiderate, unreliable, and just plain rude? Or do you assume he made every effort to get there on time but circumstances beyond his control got in his way? Maybe he was involved in an accident. Maybe he stopped to help someone in an accident. That little bit of narrative will absolutely affect your interactions with him and if you choose to be annoyed instead of gracious, he will sense it.

Consider, too, the patient that doesn't lose any weight even after you've counseled her, told her that her health problems are only going to get worse. She knows she'll need a hip or knee replacement unless she starts exercising. Every time she's in your office, her test results are more and more of a concern. Blood pressure, cholesterol, kidney and liver function all headed in the wrong direction. She's clearly not taking your advice. What story are you telling about her? She's lazy? She doesn't care about her health? She just won't put down the bag of chips or the box of cookies? One or more of these may be true, but have you found out anything about her living conditions, asked about any unresolved trauma, or learned of any family history of addiction?

It's true we tend to be much more forgiving and gracious when we learn a little bit of the why, or the story behind the story. And although you may never know the actual truth, you can choose to like your patients more when you choose to tell a different story about their behavior. They will be more likely to open up to you when they aren't sensing your judgement and disdain. And when patients like their doctors and feel that their doctors like them, they start complying more with instructions and advice.

If you want to change your patients, start by changing you.

THE CRABBY OLD LADY WHO HATES OUR FOOD

It was the end of a long week. 4:35 on a Friday afternoon and I was the only one left in the office. As I was answering the last of the email, there was a knock at my door. Four people from food service were looking for some help.

There was an older woman on one of our inpatient units who had been complaining about the food every day for the past five days. It was too cold, it was burnt, it was tasteless, it had too much salt, it was covered in grease, it was dry. You get the idea.

Normally, the dietary staff can handle those kinds of things. They've heard a complaint or two, but this woman had started to get pretty unkind to the staff and no one wanted to be the one to bring her a tray. They came to my office, hoping I might be able to talk to her.

One quick look at the clock and a heavy sigh later, and I was off to go see what I could do.

I found her nurse and told her why I was there. She rolled her eyes. "Good luck. Nothing anyone has done this week has been good enough. I think some people are just always going to be unhappy."

I walked in and found a tiny, little old lady who couldn't have weighed more than 90 pounds. I told her I was from the service excellence department and I'd heard she wasn't happy with our food. "That's an understatement," she answered.

She spent the next 15 minutes telling me about every meal she'd been served here. There was nothing on the menu that was appealing, everything was cooked incorrectly, and nobody seemed to care just how awful it all was. I listened patiently, reflected back to her what I was hearing, and told her how frustrating it must be to not be able to enjoy a meal.

She paused, looked me in the eye and asked, "Do you know why I'm here?" "No, I don't," I answered.

"I'm here because the doctors wanted to do a few more tests before they told me there's nothing they can do." She paused for a moment. "I'm going to die and I guess that's okay. I knew I would someday. But do you know what'll happen to me if I don't eat while I'm here? If I don't get enough nutrition and I'm not strong enough to be by myself, they're going to send me to a nursing home. You know what happens to people my age in nursing homes? They die. Well, I don't want to die there. I want to go home. I want to be with my family in my own bed and if I can't eat..." She stopped, took a deep breath, looked at me and said, "I need my strength. I need to eat. Do you understand?"

In that moment, the crabby old lady turned into a frail, frightened woman. I no longer found her demanding and impossible to please but vulnerable and in need of help. I set her up with some meal vouchers from our full service restaurant at the hospital (different from the hospital kitchen) and told her to contact me if she continued having trouble. I told her nurse what the real issue was, that it wasn't about the food as much as it was about her fear about dying in an institution. She shrugged, thanked me and continued charting.

I got back to my desk and even though it was well past quitting time, I was really glad I had been there. Instead of being focused on the list of things I needed to get done, I was reminded of why I do this job. I'm not there for my 'To-Do' List, I'm there for people. I don't know if she's still on this earth or if she was able to die at home, but I'm glad she had someone who listened and tried to help.

Take a few moments to find out the real issue behind the complaint. Change the story you're telling yourself about the other person. It can make all the difference. To both of you.

IT'S THE PERFECT DAY FOR A GRILLED CHEESE

He was angry. He was so angry, he got out of his hospital bed, grabbed his crutches, and walked down to administration to find the president and complain.

From his perspective, everything that could go wrong in a hospital stay had. Nothing was right. Everything was poor. He couldn't imagine how we stayed in business if this was how we treated people. A few different staff members had tried to talk with him, explain things to him, tell him that he was wrong about us, that we really are a good hospital. Nothing helped.

"Somebody call Kate."

I've been doing patient experience work for a long time so I'm used to going in and talking with people who are really upset. More often than not, I'm able to break through and resolve the situation. That day, I wasn't so sure.

When they called me, he was refusing to eat, saying that he didn't trust anything from our cafeteria. He said he had gotten so many trays of food that were wrong, he didn't think any of them would be right. And he'd complained about it so much, he thought the kitchen staff might "mess with it." Instead of trying to convince him that our staff would never do anything like that, I started by listening to him.

He told me about everything that had happened to him since he came to us, all the ways the communication had broken down, all the things that didn't go the way he thought they would. I apologized. I told him I couldn't imagine how frustrating it must be to feel like everything is going wrong. I apologized for letting him down. I didn't offer one single explanation or excuse just then, even though I could have. There were plenty of things he wasn't factually correct about but at that moment, it didn't matter. What mattered was his perception. And his perception was that we had let him down.

I asked him a few questions about his life outside of our hospital, what his life was like before he came here and learned quite a bit about him. We kept on talking about things that had nothing to do with why he was here and eventually he asked if we could step outside for a moment so he could get some fresh air. We walked outside to a very cold and rainy day, typical for the Midwest. After just a bit, it was clear that we were both getting cold so I said, "You know what I think? I think this is the perfect day for a grilled cheese sandwich. I used to love coming inside on a day like this and having a nice, hot, gooey grilled cheese sandwich. Does that sound good?"

He stared at me for a second, suspiciously. "You're thinking about it, aren't you?" I smiled.

"You know I don't trust this food here," he answered.

I said, "What if I went down there and got it so the staff thinks they're making it for me? Would that help?"

Again, he waited a moment before answering, "A grilled cheese sandwich sounds really good."

He went back up to his room and I went down to get the sandwich. I had the head of our nutrition services bring it up with me so he could see that she was on our side. We then got to talking about the problems he'd encountered and I had a chance to explain what had happened. It wasn't so much that things had gone wrong but we hadn't done as good a job as we should have in explaining those things. I tried to make it clear I wasn't making excuses, just trying to reassure him that he was safe, no one had messed up, but we needed to be better about communicating. He smiled and not only ate the sandwich, but ordered dinner and breakfast for the next morning. Success.

The next day, he was cleared for discharge and before he left, he asked to see me. I went up to his room to make sure everything was in order and to ensure he knew what to do once he got home. He thanked me, took my hands and brought his head down so his forehead was on them, stayed there a moment, and kissed my hand. "This place needs you," he said. "I appreciate you and everything you did for me. Thank you."

It was the perfect day for a grilled cheese.

DIFFICULT PATIENTS

I've written before about patients who are 'difficult' or 'impossible to please,' and I usually conclude by asking you to tell a different story about that patient. Get to know them. Ask them a little about what they're going through. Find out the back story that's causing them to act that way. I still stand behind that, but I think there may be another element at work here.

Each of us wants to do a good job. We want to go home at the end of the day knowing that we made a difference, made someone's life better, helped someone. When we can't do it, it's easier to blame the patients than ourselves.

When we have so many things to do, demands to meet, meetings to attend, call lights to answer; when we didn't get enough sleep the night before, had an argument with our spouse that morning, or are struggling with a difficult personal issue; when we've reached our limit and just can't do one more thing to help, we call a patient 'difficult.'

I know I do it when a person has a complaint about something and I'm genuinely at a loss as to how to fix it. I like to think I'm good at my job so when someone brings me an issue I don't know how to solve, it's hard for me to imagine that the problem lies in me. I'd much rather believe the problem is with them.

Don't get me wrong; I'm sure there are plenty of people out there who really are difficult, who really are hard to please, and who really are attention-seeking. The key in caring for them is not to let that stop us from trying. Difficult patients still need their call light answered, still need to be assisted to the restroom, and still need their questions answered.

As for what we can learn from patients like this, I think they can make us better at our jobs. It's easy to be nice to patients who are nice; it's much harder to be nice to patients who are more demanding. I've learned how to be better at not getting defensive, I've learned patience, I've learned how to ask questions that go deeper to try to get at the root of what's really bothering them. These are all skills I can apply to my personal life, too.

Admittedly, I still have a lot of work to do to get better at these things, but I wouldn't have gotten these skills at all if every patient I'd encountered had been sweet. Think about the backstory of your difficult patient, yes, and also think about what they may be teaching you about you.

ALL IT TAKES IS ONE

A few years ago, I was in charge of reviewing all of the social media posts about our hospital. I sifted through everything on Facebook, Yelp, Google +, and the like and added those comments to our tracking and trending forms of what was being said about us. That, along with our comments from the surveys, helped us determine which areas were doing great and which needed a little extra assistance.

One comment that stands out in my memory was a 5-star Yelp review from a woman who was over the moon about the great care she'd gotten in our Emergency Department. She'd written several paragraphs, each one more glowing than the last, about all the wonderful people who had cared for her, how quickly she'd been seen, and how this was her hospital of choice, despite living closer to our competitor.

She had a list of nurses' and physicians' names and showered praise over each of them, likening them to gods and angels. It was quite a review.

I remember sending it to the team; the ED wasn't accustomed to hearing good news. More often than not, when people post on social media it's to complain and trash-talk (often anonymously). So I was happy in this case to send over something to brighten their day.

Not 72 hours later, she posted again, this time calling us THE WORST HOSPITAL EVER (emphasis hers) and warning people to never go there. EVER. She got my attention.

I took a walk over to the ED and asked what had happened at her last visit, why she had gone from our #1 fan to our biggest hater.

As it turns out, there was one person with whom she'd interacted and it didn't go well. It wasn't so much a negative interaction as it was a just-not-quite-as-good-as-the-previous-ones kind of interaction. We'd done such an impressive job earlier, that we set the bar pretty high. This staff member wasn't quite as attentive and it set us back. A lot.

I thought long and hard about how to handle this. She'd left her name, so it wouldn't have been inappropriate for us to contact her. Should I call her? Should the manager of the ED call her? Should the person she'd complained about call her?

Ultimately, I did. I was used to these kinds of conversations and it was certainly in my job description to follow up on reviews, positive or negative. I braced myself and dialed her number.

She picked up on the first ring and, after I introduced myself, went into a tirade about how completely awful and disappointing we were. I listened, didn't interrupt or try to apologize at first. Just let her talk. And talk she did.

"It sounds like this visit was very different from the others," were my first words after she'd finished. "I'm so sorry. I can hear how disappointed you are."

SECTION FIVE: THE PATIENT STORIES

"You're damn right I am," she continued. I let her continue. She said mostly the same things she'd said before, but it clearly mattered to her that I heard them.

"Gloria (not her real name), I'm so sorry we let you down. You came to expect a certain level of care and service from us and we didn't deliver this time. I'm sorry we missed the mark the other day. What can we do moving forward?"

After a few seconds of silence she said, "Nothing. It's in the past. But I'm glad you called."

"Gloria, I hope it's not any time soon, but if you ever need to go to an emergency department again, whether it's here or another hospital, I hope you receive the level of care you expected from us."

"Well, I know you guys can do it. You did it before, you can do it again." She paused. "I love your hospital. I don't want to go anywhere else. But you have to do better, okay? I know you can do better. Promise me you'll do better."

I thanked her for talking with me and she thanked me for calling her. I was glad I did. Until that call, I don't think I realized that people really do form relationships with their hospitals. This was her hospital. It was familiar. She felt safe there. We needed to reassure her that this one bad experience was not going to be the new normal.

All it takes is one bad interaction. It can completely undo all the goodwill you've built up with your community. If you're lucky enough to get the opportunity to apologize, don't pass it up.

A TALE OF
TWO HOSPITALIZATIONS

A few months ago, before just about everything was shut down due to COVID-19, a good friend of mine was suffering with some horrible, and all too familiar pain. He knew he had a kidney stone and went to the nearby emergency department to get some relief.

After a few hours and several imaging tests, the news wasn't good. The stones were too big to pass and he needed surgery to have them removed. The physician went ahead and admitted him, hoping the surgery could be done in the morning.

Although it was located in the middle of nowhere, this hospital had recently been acquired by a larger health system, one with a wonderful reputation in the community, not only for clinical excellence, but for exceptional patient care. I felt relieved that he was in good hands.

We spoke about a week and a half later. As it turned out, he didn't have the surgery at that hospital. He had been there for a few days, waiting, but was unexpectedly released. His daughter then brought him to the hospital near her.

"What on earth happened?" I asked him.

"I have no idea," he answered. "The whole time I was there, I didn't know what the hell was going on. There didn't appear to be any coordination or communication between any of the staff, like nobody was running the ship, and plenty of conflicting information."

He continued. "They wouldn't let me eat anything because I was waiting for an OR, which was understandable, but this went on for two days. I kept asking when I'd be going in to have these stones removed, and no one had an answer. Then, finally, they took me down to surgery and the doctor came in and said I was getting a stent."

"A stent?" I asked. "Why not remove the stones?"

"That's exactly what I asked," he answered. "Something about them not having the equipment to be able to do it, but they were telling me this while I was lying on a gurney right outside the OR. The whole time I was on the unit, I kept hearing them talk about removal. No one said anything about a stent"

"Afterwards," he continued, "they gave me a prescription for some pain pills and told me to make an appointment for a follow up visit in two weeks. That was it. I felt like I was getting the 'bum's rush' out of there. My daughter was furious and took me directly to the hospital near her and that's when everything changed."

"What happened there?" I asked. I had a feeling I knew what he was going to say.

"The physician there was amazing. He was confident without being arrogant and at some point he put his hand on my shoulder and said, 'It's okay. Everything is going to be fine.' That felt great. Very reassuring. It was like night and day between those two places."

He went on to tell me that it felt like everything was running smoothly; everyone knew the plan of care, and he never felt like he was being a bother when he asked for help. He even noticed that behind everyone's ID badge, there was a plastic card listing 'Always Behaviors', similar to AIDET, something he'd heard me talk about a lot.

As happy as I was for him that he got the care he needed and was just fine, I was a little disappointed. I was really hoping for something new, some magic nugget of information that would turn the patient experience movement on its ear. Something we never knew, never tried. Something revolutionary that would solve it all.

Alas, it all came down to the same old things: listen well, communicate clearly, convey kindness. All those things we've been talking about and training on for years. No new shiny bit of technology, nothing terribly complicated.

It really can be that simple.

DO WE *REALLY* KNOW WHAT'S BEST FOR OUR PATIENTS?

Back in the mid 1990's – early 2000's, I worked for the organization that coordinated all of the organ donations and transplants in Illinois. I met with families who had a loved one in the ICU, often due to an unexpected trauma like a car accident or gunshot wound, and asked them to consider donating that loved one's organs to save someone else's life. A tough job, to be sure, but one I found truly rewarding.

While I learned a lot about the medical side of donation – the Glasgow Coma Scale, the importance of vasopressors, and how to do an apnea test – I learned a lot more about human nature; how quickly we form opinions about people and how those opinions are often completely wrong.

It was a Saturday night in the summer, our busiest time. My pager (yes, pager, it was a long time ago) went off just before midnight and I was sent to Cook County Hospital. The old Cook County Hospital, before the much-prettier Stroger building. There was a 21-year-old man there who had just been transferred from the Cook County jail. The other inmates had quite literally beaten the life out of him.

Now at this point, I'll tell you that he was African-American and that's actually relevant because it was our practice to send an African-American staff person to approach African-American families. However, that night, they were either post-call or on another case and I was the next one up. I hadn't had very many opportunities to work with families who were of a different race and I just wasn't sure how this was going to go.

I got to the hospital and there in the dimly lit room was his family, about 20 women who were praying and crying and waiting for some definitive news from the doctors. The neurosurgery resident was about to go in and tell the family that, despite their best efforts, he was brain dead. He wanted me to go in with him and ask the family about donating his organs. We never like to have those conversations together; it's best to let people come to terms with what brain dead means and later present donation as a next step, once they're ready. But that wasn't going to happen that night.

The resident gathered everyone together at the bedside (another thing we don't generally like) and broke the news: the young man had died. Immediately, the mother fell to the floor, crying, screaming. The others circled around her, fanning her face, giving her juice, praying. When she came to her feet she said, "I need to go home. Get me out of this hospital. My baby's dead. I need to get out of here!" Her family was helping her to the door, when the chaplain said, "Wait a moment, this lady has something she wants to ask you." She looked at me and said, "Go ahead, ask."

I shot that chaplain a look like I was trying to burn a hole into her, eyes wide and subtly trying to shake my head no. This was clearly not the time. The mother looked at me with unimaginable pain on her face and said, "What? What could you possibly have to ask me? I just need to go home!"

With all the courage I could muster, certain that these women were going to start swinging, I squeaked out the words, "Organ donation. Unique position. Help someone. Maybe?"

I braced myself, ready to hear a stream of obscenities, and started to look for another way out of that room, when the mother got on her feet, looked me right in the face and said, "You're telling me my boy could save someone's life?" "Yes, ma'am," I answered, still not sure what she was going to do.

Suddenly everything changed. The room erupted in cries of, "Hallelujah! Praise Jesus! My baby's going to save someone's life!" There was singing, there was hugging, there was laughter through all the tears. The mother signed my consent form and couldn't wait to hear about how her son's organs were going to be used to help people.

I was stunned. This was the very last thing I thought would happen.

Imagine what that family's night would have been like if I had not been pressured by that chaplain, if I'd gone with my gut, decided it wasn't a good time, and left the hospital labeling this family "Unapproachable." They would have gone home feeling just as terrible, just as heartbroken. They would have had no hope, nothing to help them get through this awful event. All because I thought I knew what was best for them. By not asking, I would have made the decision for them. And it would have been the wrong decision.

When I think about how we as healthcare workers make decisions for patients – usually with the best of intentions – I wonder just how often we end up doing more harm than good. We make assumptions about people and think we're acting in their best interests when, in fact, we should be letting them make those important decisions for themselves. We can assist, guide, educate, and support but we should never do it for them.

I try to remind myself of this family every time I think I know how people are going to react to things. The story I tell myself about people isn't the *real* story and learning to recognize that has been one of the most important lessons I've learned when it comes to making a genuine connection with people.

SHOW COMPASSION TO A MURDERER

Child abuse. We all hated those cases. Years ago, when I was working in the organ donation and transplantation industry, I was called out to a case involving child abuse. As you might imagine, it was incredibly difficult to see a small child injured to such an extent as to cause brain death, but the added layer of knowing the death was caused by a parent or caregiver was often too much to take. Most of us required a lot of de-briefing and assistance as we processed our emotions after a case.

In this particular instance, the mother of the child was the one suspected of perpetrating the abuse. Because there was no definitive proof yet, she and her husband were the ones I had to approach to obtain consent for organ and tissue donation.

I walked onto the pediatric intensive care unit and found the RN who was caring for the little girl. She was visibly upset. She had been caring for this child for several days and watched her neurologic decline until a declaration of brain death had been made. She pulled me aside and told me the parents weren't right.

"What do you mean 'not right'?"

"Mom is not behaving like a normal grieving mother," she answered. "And dad has some cognitive deficits, like he's developmentally delayed. The whole thing is a mess." Her voice broke and she looked like she was fighting back tears. She walked away before I could ask her anything more.

I went and took the parents to a small conference room and began as I always did. "What have the doctors told you about your daughter's condition?"

"They said she's dead." Mom's response had an alarmingly flat affect. I had talked to many parents who had lost their children and I've seen several who were trying to be very matter-of-fact and hold themselves together but you could hear the pain behind their voices. They were devastated but trying to get through what they knew they needed to get through at the hospital.

This one was different. There was no emotion behind her eyes.

As we talked about the option of organ donation, I felt a tingle running up and down my spine. "Something's wrong," I thought. "This isn't shock or a delayed response. What is this?"

She asked a lot of questions about the surgery and what organs and tissues could be donated. I took my time and answered as thoroughly and compassionately as I could. She told me that the staff at the hospital hadn't been very nice to her; they were convinced she had hurt her daughter and she said she trusted me. I told her she *could* trust me. We would take excellent care of her daughter's body during the donation process and would let her know all about the recipients of her life-saving gift.

She hugged me. And that's when my blood ran cold. I actually felt a chill when she put her arms around me.

"This woman doesn't feel anything." The voice inside my head felt she had, in fact, done horrible, unspeakable things to her daughter. That I had positioned myself as someone she could trust was more than I could take.

We got the paperwork signed and I called the procurement team in to get started on the process. The mother's sister came up to me and thanked me for showing her sister such compassion and respect.

"We've always known there was something different about my sister," she began. "She didn't express or exhibit emotions like other people. Growing up, I remember her always looking around and then doing what everyone else was doing, especially when it came to feelings. Thank you for not judging her, but treating her kindly. She never would have agreed to donate organs if you hadn't been kind to her."

I was speechless, overwhelmed with all that had happened, sad to see this three-year-old's life come to an end, and feeling like I had betrayed her somehow by being nice to her mother, the person who I suspected killed her.

I made my way to the staff break room and couldn't hold back my emotions anymore. I cried. I'd never done that on a case before. They train us to keep our emotions in check and not get consumed by the tragedy that often accompanies a brain death diagnosis. But I couldn't contain myself. I felt horrible. One of the nurses came in and I tried to pull myself together, not wanting to look vulnerable or unprofessional in front of her.

"It's okay," she said. "It's actually good to see this. We kinda think of you donation guys as vultures. It's good to know you feel things like we do."

The donation process began and this little girl was able to save a number of people's lives. I don't know what came of the mother, whether criminal charges were filed, or if she was convicted. What I do know is that it took me a very long time to process my feelings. I had never come face to face with what appeared to be a real-life antisocial personality disorder. It's something I'd seen in movies and heard about on the news. I lived in Chicago, after all, the land of John Wayne Gacy who had committed the most atrocious acts imaginable on young boys. But I'd never spoken to or been hugged by a person who was completely void of emotion. It was bone-chilling.

Over time, I've come to realize that this was a person with a disease. Just like someone with diabetes or multiple sclerosis, she didn't *choose* to be this way. She deserved my compassion and mercy just as anyone else with a disease would.

It's a lot more difficult to remember that when a person has committed unspeakable acts of violence on a child, but that's really what's at the heart of healthcare, isn't it? People come to us needing our help and it's not our job to pass judgement; it's our job to serve. We need to leave judgement to law enforcement and the courts. Our job is to care, to minister, to serve, to show compassion and mercy. Remember that the next time you're faced with a difficult or even unspeakable case. And if you're struggling, reach out for help. You don't need to try to process those feelings alone.

THE FAMILY CONFERENCE

I hadn't been involved in the case. I didn't know anything about why the family was upset, only that their father had died and they had questions about what had happened.

I met the patient's two adult daughters in the hospital lobby and escorted them back to our conference room where several staff members, including the hospitalist physician who had cared for him, were waiting. After we'd gone around the table and introduced ourselves, I asked the daughters to tell us about their concerns.

As they told their story, I looked around the table and took note of how we were sitting, where our hands were, what kinds of expressions were on our faces. Most of us were sitting forward in our chairs, hands together, eyes on the sisters, while periodically nodding our heads or pursing our lips as they spoke. The hospitalist sat back in his chair, arms folded across his chest, looking mostly at the table. The sisters noticed.

"Why can't you look at me?" one of them demanded. "I've been asking questions about what happened and all you can do is stare down at the papers in front of you."

He looked startled. "I just want to be sure I'm answering your questions accurately. I printed parts of his record so I don't say anything incorrect."

I could appreciate where he was coming from; he came to the family conference prepared to answer medical questions about what had happened. He didn't come prepared to address their feelings about what had happened.

The woman continued, "All of you at this table have offered an apology and I believe everyone here feels genuinely sorry. Except you." I shifted uncomfortably in my chair as she pointed at him.

"Maybe you do feel bad. Maybe you do have some empathy for me and my sister but you need to learn how to make people see that. I don't believe for one second that you care at all and I really hope I'm wrong. If you really do care, then don't just say you're sorry. Show it."

I was starting to feel really bad for him. Here he was in a room with several staff members, including the Chief Medical Officer, getting raked over the coals for a death that really wasn't his fault. And that's where he was stuck – it wasn't my fault.

I've said before that patients and their families don't really care whose fault something is. They just want to know you heard them, you're sorry, and you'll do your best to be sure it doesn't happen again. In this case, the patient's daughters wanted medical answers, yes, but they also wanted all of us to understand how difficult things had been and to take steps to improve. This poor guy was stuck.

As uncomfortable as this family conference was, I'm very glad we had it. It gave all of us at the table a chance to hear directly from the family how scary, confusing, and frustrating it can be when loved ones are in our care. We forget sometimes that treating a patient also means caring for a family, and that showing genuine empathy involves more than simply saying you're sorry.

CLEAR IS KIND, PART ONE

I read a lot of Brené Brown's work. Her book, The Gifts of Imperfection, made a huge impact on me and I've been a fan of hers ever since it came out in 2010. I've started reading her most recent work, Dare to Lead, and in it, she talks about how being clear is kind.

It made me think back to when I was working in organ donation and transplantation. I was not on the recipient side, where the person who has been sick for so long finally gets that life-saving transplant. I was on the donor side, where a family who has just suffered a sudden tragedy is asked to make the ultimate selfless decision and donate their loved one's organs.

Since most Americans hate to think of death, we tend to use phrases like 'passed on,' 'is no longer with us,' or 'is in a better place.' They told us on day one of orientation NOT to use euphemisms. Say 'dead' or 'died.' It may be uncomfortable for you as the bearer of bad news, but it's the kindest thing you can do. Families will appreciate it.

I said it a lot. I got used to saying it and I got used to hearing it.

Fast-forward a few years to when my husband and I were throwing a party at my house around the 4th of July. All of our friends and family were there, including my very best friend. It was well into the evening and many of us had had a few too many drinks, so when her phone rang and I saw all the color drain from her face, I didn't know what had happened.

I heard her say her brother's name. I heard the word hospital. I thought I'd heard accident, but I wasn't sure. I looked to my other friend in the room. "Wait… what happened? Is he okay?"

"He's fine now," she said.

"Oh, thank God," I answered. "Something happened but he's okay?"

"He's much better now. He's out of pain."

"Wait. Is he okay or is he not okay?" I struggled to read her face and make some sense of the situation. My best friend had run out of the room crying and saying she had to get to the hospital, but my other friend was calmly telling me he was better. I had no idea what was what and those moments of uncertainty were horrible.

Finally, my husband, who hadn't had a single drink, said, "He died, Kate. We have to get her to the hospital so she can be with the rest of her family. Let's go. I'm driving."

And at that moment, I understood. As horrible and unthinkable as that news was, I was almost relieved to know what we were dealing with. The next few days were a terrible blur for all of us, but I kept going back to those first moments when everything was so confusing.

I suppose it's easier to deal with being mad at the one being unclear than it is to deal with your feelings about a friend dying. But when you're faced with a sudden, unexpected, and tragic loss, what you need is information. Clarity.

I know when Brené Brown says "clear is kind" she's talking about instructions, feedback, expectations generally between co-workers or bosses and employees. But it's also true in painful situations like death. While we may want to soften the blow and use those phrases we think are helpful, it really only makes things worse.

When I'm talking to an angry patient and trying to do some service recovery, the very best thing I can do besides apologize is be very clear about what happened and what we're going to do about it. Patients want answers and, as uncomfortable as it can be for me, it doesn't pay to use fluffy language to try and soften things up.

Clear is kind.

CLEAR IS KIND, PART TWO

Last time, I wrote about Brené Brown and how she stresses that clear is kind. I related it to my own experiences surrounding death and dying and, while using language like *passed on to a better place* may feel more comfortable, it isn't clear. And it isn't kind.

Thinking about all that reminded me of another incident in which being clear would have been much kinder.

I was working at a smaller community hospital, not a large trauma or academic medical center, when a patient who'd had multiple cardiac arrests on the floor was moved to the Intensive Care Unit with a significant decrease in brain function. The family was understandably upset and wanted answers about how this happened.

We needed to have a family conference but there were no conference rooms available at that moment. We did the next best thing and gathered in the empty patient room next to his while the team of physicians and nurses spoke with the family about what had happened and what the plan was, moving forward.

In hindsight, it's easy now to see where we went wrong. We allowed the family to remain in that empty patient room after the conference. We thought we were being sensitive and accommodating, but over the next several days, they had multiple family members round the clock, sleeping in sleeping bags on the floor of that room. They brought in coolers filled with water and juice and even plugged in a crock pot for pulled pork sandwiches.

We thought that by not setting any boundaries, we were being nice but it was the worst thing we could have done. By not telling them at 9pm that it was time to go home, we gave them the message that they shouldn't leave. They stayed and didn't get the rest they needed. They even asked if they could use the patient showers so they could clean up.

It also put an undue burden on the staff. There was a window between the two rooms so anytime a nurse went into his room to provide care, the family was watching. It was very hard for the nurses to focus and concentrate, knowing that there were people looking at them. People who, quite frankly, didn't really know what they were looking at.

This went on for over a week before the patient was transferred to a hospital that could offer a higher level of care. That place, I knew, had very clear boundaries about how many visitors could be there at any given time, very clear visiting hours, and a very strict no crock pot policy.

It's important to remember that the things we say or do when we try to be sensitive or accommodating aren't always the kindest. Families need to know it's okay to go home. To sleep in their own bed. To shower in their own bathroom. Or if they live out of town, at least at a hotel. Somewhere that isn't the hospital so they can recharge, refresh, and be ready to support the patient and each other.

This is where being a patient experience professional can get a little tricky. For those of us who have a hard time saying no, saying yes to every request seems like the kind thing to do. It isn't. Not always. We have to stress the importance of downtime, of rest, and we have to be sure we've earned their trust, so they know they can leave the room and their loved one will still be safe.

I wish we'd done things differently for that family. I wish I'd known of Brené Brown and her *clear is kind* message at that point in my career. It would have been a much kinder situation for everyone.

SECTION SIX:
THE FIRST
PERSON STORIES

I think it would be impossible to write about my work in patient experience without also including what it's like as a patient or, as is more often the case with me, the family member of a patient.

When you train people to deliver exceptional service, you really notice when it's not there. If I walk up to a reception desk and have to wait for the conversion about last night's episode of The Bachelor to end before I'm acknowledged, we're going to have a problem. And on the other hand, when you know how busy and stressful it can get, you tend to offer a little more grace when you see how hard the team is working.

The real issue though, is that my professional hat goes right out the window when I'm scared. As hard as I try to remember to ask all the right questions and take all the right notes and remember all the discharge instructions, I can't. In those moments, I'm not a healthcare professional; I'm a patient, a daughter, a sister, a wife, a mom. It's not just another day at the office anymore. Everything looks different.

You search for kind eyes, for someone who will take an extra moment to be sure you understand what just happened, for someone who looks at you and really sees you, not just your disease, for someone who understands how scared you are and doesn't make you feel like you're a bother.

I hate to think that you need to go through something like that yourself in order to exhibit that level of compassion and empathy. But I did. As caring as I was in my mid-20s, it wasn't at the level it is now, after having lost three family members in 3 years. I remember what it felt like to be ignored, passed off to someone else, minimized, frustrated, helpless. More importantly, I know it when I see it in others and it moves me to action.

The young workforce has the best of intentions, I'm sure, but experiencing a health crisis changes you. You can't help but see those patient faces differently, to know how it feels to be so desperately in need of help, kindness, information, and guidance. You just want to make things better.

So here they are, the first person stories, what it felt like to be on the other side, my 'why' behind what I do.

WHEN YOU'RE THE PATIENT

Whether it's organ transplant, physician relations, or patient experience, I've spent my entire career working in and around hospitals. It's been pretty normal for me to go to a hospital five days a week, for nine or ten hours a day. I know there are people who are terrified of hospitals, who believe that's where people go to die, but I've never really had a fear of them.

I've observed a few surgeries, been to hundreds of medical centers, visited thousands of physician offices, served on dozens of hospital committees, and worked in the operational and administrative sides of healthcare. I've also been the person who goes with the friend or family member when they have an appointment to ask the right questions, write things down, offer support and comfort, all of that. It's old hat to me. Not a problem, of course I'll go with you.

None of that prepared me for what it feels like to be the patient.

My routine mammogram turned into a breast MRI, which led to an ultrasound, which led to a biopsy. Given my wide-spread and always fatal family history of cancer (both grandmothers, a grandfather, my mom, my dad, and my sister) I was petrified. I'd been kind of joking about it for years; it's coming for me, it's only a matter of time; but there was nothing funny about going through all these tests just waiting to hear how far along it had gotten or what stage it was in or how long I had...

I'd recently moved halfway across the country and had only been living in the area for about a year and hadn't yet gotten to know all the players at the hospital where I was having all these tests. I didn't yet know who the best of the best physicians were. There was no one I knew well enough to fully trust.

And one question kept coming up in my head at every encounter: do they have any idea how terrified I am?

Every scheduling phone call, every check-in at the desk, every assistant who walked me to an exam room, every tech who performed a test, every physician who offered an inconclusive result. Do they have any idea how terrified I am? Do they know my family history? Do they know that I'm worried about my daughter, too? Do they know that in my family there is no such thing as a cancer survivor? Do they know how scared I am?

I think a few of them did. They were kind, patient, gentle. But to others, I think I was just another procedure to do. It made me wonder if I'm looking at the people who come in and out of my workplace every day with that same sense of routine. It's a hospital, it's my work, it's no big deal.

After this experience, I will not see it that way again. Hospitals are scary for some. We can't possibly know all the history our visitors bring with them. What we have to know is how to be kind, patient, gentle. Every patient. Every time.

FROM THE OTHER SIDE

Recently, I had to undergo some surgery. Routine, standard stuff but it did require me to be completely knocked out for a few hours with the possibility of an overnight stay. I'd never gone through anything like that before, so I had my share of nerves the morning of the procedure.

My surgeon doesn't practice at the hospital in which I work; she's at the smaller hospital near my home, which was actually a good thing. People were telling me that the car ride home was going to be tough; I'd feel every bump, every sudden stop, every pot hole in the road, so it was best that the drive home was 20 minutes instead of 75.

Before things got started in the operating room, I was watching everyone. The staff at this hospital didn't know that I worked in Service Excellence and Patient Experience at the big hospital up the road. To them, I was just another person in need of care. To me, I was kind of a mystery shopper. I was keeping track of how people were introducing themselves to me, how well they explained what was going to happen, how accommodating they were to my husband who was with me, everything. They were great. I even remember that there was Beatles music playing, which helped calm me down even more. All you need is love.

I remember my surgeon coming in ahead of time to check in on me and answer any last minute questions. Same with the anesthesiologist; he came by to make sure I was okay before we went into the OR.

The next thing I knew, it was several hours later. The surgery lasted about an hour longer than expected and it took me a while to wake up. The post-op nurse took out the IV in my left hand and told me it was time to get dressed (I don't actually remember that part) but I do remember my husband trying to help me get my shoes on and feeling very dizzy and light-headed and needing to lie back down.

It was some time later and I was still feeling like the room was spinning. The nurse that was caring for me told my husband that they were filling up in post-op so I needed to start getting ready to go home. I don't know what he said, but the next thing I knew, there was a new nurse in the room who put in a new IV into my other hand. I heard something about "getting her some fluids" and a short time later, I was feeling a whole lot better. Still sleepy and kind of out of it, but not dizzy anymore.

With that, I was in a wheelchair, then my car, then home. A few days later when I wasn't sleeping 18+ hours each day, I started to remember more and more details about that day. I remember everyone being really nice and helpful, but my husband will tell you about the nurse who wasn't picking up on my physical cues and seemed more focused on clearing the bed than making sure I was well enough to go home. He felt a lot better when the new nurse showed up and took action, but the moments leading up to that are the parts of the story he remembers more than any of the other really good things that happened that day.

Patient Experience is a team sport; all it takes is one misstep for the lasting impression to be less than excellent. And it affects more than just the patient, especially when the patient is unconscious for a period of time. Making sure that family members are well-informed and feel comfortable advocating for their loved one is just as important as direct patient care.

When asked, he and I tell a slightly different story about how things went that day, but what our stories have in common is that most of the staff was kind, responsive, and showed genuine concern for me. And that's a great patient story.

TWO TRIPS TO THE URGENT CARE

This past week, I found myself in the throws of one of the worst head colds I've had in quite some time. I don't get sick easily; all the years of working in hospitals has made my immune system pretty tough, so when I do get sick, it's usually something major. I had been a little congested for a few days, but woke up one morning with an excruciating sore throat that made it nearly impossible to swallow. My primary care physician didn't have an opening for me that day and I simply couldn't wait to get some relief so off I went to the local urgent care clinic in town.

I got in almost immediately and saw the nurse practitioner. She was great. Very kind, very thorough, and very sympathetic to my pain. My rapid strep test came back negative (surprisingly) as did the influenza test, so she didn't want to prescribe antibiotics but, rather, manage my symptoms. That made sense to me. All I really wanted was some relief from the throat pain.

I picked up the prescription for viscous lidocaine, which did help the sore throat but tasted like motor oil, and I stayed in bed for the next two days.

BETTER THAN I FOUND IT

I started to feel like I was getting better but three days later, not only was my sore throat back with a vengeance, but now my right ear felt like someone was sticking knives in it. My husband said I turned an eerie shade of white and insisted we get back to the urgent care right away. I didn't argue.

We arrived 10 minutes prior to closing time and the reception-ist told us they weren't taking any more patients. I told her I had been there a few days ago and my symptoms had gotten worse. She apolo-gized and said we could either come back in the morning or go to the Emergency Department tonight. The ED for a sore throat? No way.

I was contemplating how many boxes of popsicles to buy to hold me over until morning when my husband suggested the urgent care about a half an hour away, which was open later. As much as I'm a fan of continuity of care, I knew there weren't enough popsicles in the whole town to get me through the night so off we went.

The other urgent care center doesn't look like much from the road, but inside it's quite lovely. The receptionist was very nice, as was the tech who took my vitals, but the real star was the nurse prac-titioner. Her main concern was getting me some immediate relief, especially after she learned that I'd been suffering for nearly a week. She gave me a steroid, decadron, along with an antibiotic for the ear infection I'd developed. By the time I picked up a box of popsicles at the grocery down the street, I was feeling 100% better.

I slept better that night than I had in several days and the pain in my throat never returned. It was amazing. That shot of decadron may have been slightly outside the usual course of treatment, but it was exactly what I needed.

I'm not saying anything bad about the first center; she did exactly what she should have. No antibiotics for a virus, I get it. But when it comes to relieving suffering, the second center knew just what to do.

Incidentally, I asked them how close to closing time they stop seeing patients. The tech said they don't turn anyone away if they get there before 7pm. Even if it's 6:59, if they need care, they get it that night. Admittedly, it can get a little tough on staff who are eager to get home after a 10-hour day, but the mission, the reason they're there, is what keeps them going. They know they are there to help. And they do.

PRIVACY ISSUES

A couple of weeks ago, I had to take my husband in for an outpatient surgical procedure at the main campus of our local hospital. Everywhere I looked, there were posted signs about treating patients with courtesy, respect, and caring. The hospital's mission statement was on every computer screen and the staff were among some of the friendliest I'd ever encountered.

The whole time he was in surgery, I felt very comfortable that they were taking excellent care of him.

While he was coming out of anesthesia in post-op, I went back there to check on him and noticed the computer on wheels next to him had his chart up on the screen. Before I had a chance to really study it (which, by the way, I shouldn't be able to), they wheeled another patient in and pulled the curtain between them for privacy. In doing so, however, the computer with his chart on the screen ended up on the other side of the curtain.

I asked the nurse about it. "That computer has my husband's medical record up on the screen and it's with that other patient."

She didn't flinch. "Well, that patient isn't even awake yet so it's not an issue."

She didn't move the computer, she didn't close his record, she didn't do anything except tell me I didn't need to worry about it. And at that moment, I was so focused on helping my husband get oriented, I didn't challenge her or insist she take some action. But it's been nagging at me...

Years ago, when I first started conducting patient experience training, I emphasized that delivering an exceptional experience is so much more than just 'being nice'. Among the many components is building trust. This nurse chipped away at trust by leaving my husband's chart up on the screen and did away with it entirely by not addressing my concern. All the posted signs about courtesy and caring meant nothing to me at that point.

Patient experience is *everything* a patient experiences. Our initial greeting, our explanations of procedures, our signage, our website, our parking, our respect for privacy, the way we handle concerns and complaints, all of it and so much more shapes the way our patients see us. It all influences whether they'll come back to us or choose our competitor down the street.

As for my husband and I, I'm not sure where we'll go next time. It'll take a lot more than friendliness for this hospital to win back my trust.

WHEN YOUR SPOUSE IS THE PATIENT

"Honey. Honey, wake up.
We have to go to the hospital right now."

My husband has had his share of health problems, but I'll never get used to being awakened from a sound sleep to those words.

I somehow managed to get myself out of bed, brush my teeth, and throw on some clothes before braving the several feet of snow and merciless winter wind to get to the car. As he was doubled over in pain in the passenger seat, I pulled out of the driveway, into the dark and headed toward the local emergency department.

Walking in the front door toward the registration desk, I took notice of everything around us. Having worked at my share of hospitals, I was on high alert. Was the person at the desk looking up as we walked in? Was the waiting area clean? Were there signs telling us where to go and what we needed to do? I noticed everything.

It's funny how we're so much more vigilant when it's a loved one as opposed to ourselves.

I got him over to the front desk and smiled when the woman told us her name and said she was going to walk us through the registration process. She was patient while he took a few extra moments to pull his wallet from his back pocket. The pain in his stomach made it hard for him to straighten up but she didn't seem to mind.

We got back to the treatment area almost immediately and I noticed that everyone we passed on the way to his room acknowledged us in some way, whether it was a smile, a hello, or just eye contact. I started to relax. A little.

It wasn't long before the physician came in and asked one simple open-ended question, "Hello, Mr. Kalthoff. What brings you in tonight?"

Anyone who knows my husband knows he can't ever answer a question with a simple answer. If you ask him what time it is, you'll learn all about the history of watchmaking.

I watched this doctor's face as he relayed his entire medical history and that of his father's and was truly impressed that she didn't interrupt. She asked very focused questions to get him back on track but it never came off as rude or impatient. That's a skill I could use, especially when I ask what he'd like for dinner.

She got to the heart of the medical issue that brought him to the ER and in no time he was back in imaging getting a CT scan. They even let me go back with him, which I didn't expect, and told us it would be about an hour before we'd get some results. I looked at the clock and started the countdown.

While we waited, several people came in to check on him, including a student who had anticipatory service down to an art. Without having to ask, she brought me a glass of water and a pillow for the uncomfortable chair I'd been sitting in and an extra blanket for my husband. I was impressed. He was oblivious. The pain meds had kicked in.

Which brings me to the point. Often, patients don't notice the things family members notice. And even if they do, they're less likely to be upset by them. I can make excuses for doctors and nurses all day if I'm the patient, but if it's my family, that protective instinct kicks in and I'm ready for battle.

Thankfully, that night in the emergency department, there was no battle needed. Everyone was marvelous. The CT results came back sooner than expected and his condition was explained in a way we both could understand. We left feeling much better than we did when we came in and I happily filled out the survey when it came a few days later in the mail.

When we talk about patient experience, we cannot forget the people who are with them. They notice everything. They worry more. They have more questions. They listen closely to how their loved one is spoken to or spoken about. We have to remember to include them in the discussion and address their needs, as well.

ARE WE TREATING THE DISEASE OR THE PERSON?

In 2008, my family got the worst news we could imagine; mom was diagnosed with breast cancer. Although true to her stoic Norwegian roots, she was appropriately nervous about what lay ahead. Her mom had died from breast cancer just a few years before and she'd seen all that she had gone through. But my mom was determined to win.

She found an oncologist that she really liked, something I knew was important. After nearly 50 years as a Registered Nurse, mom had a great deal of respect for physicians. She didn't *like* all of them, but she knew how much training they'd had, how much knowledge they had to keep at the top of their minds, how much pressure they were under all the time. She admired them. And she never, ever questioned them. So when she found this oncologist and hit it off with her immediately, I was happy. She had a lot of respect for her and I know it made a difference in her mindset when battling this disease.

Mom did well. She fought for about a year, after which she looked to be free and clear. We all breathed a sigh of relief and went on with life.

A year later at one of her follow up visits, we got sucker-punched. The cancer had returned and had metastasized to her liver. This time, her oncologist had a different treatment plan, something much more aggressive. Mom was totally on board. She liked this physician, trusted her, and would have done whatever she said.

In just a few short months we saw a dramatic difference. Mom was weak, her skin was yellow, she couldn't eat. She wasn't at all the same and she looked like she was getting worse every week. I was working at another hospital as the Physician Relations Manager and had gotten to know a couple of the oncologists there. I asked mom if she'd consider going to one of them for a second opinion on her treatment options.

"No. Absolutely not. I like this doctor. I trust her. I'm not going to anyone else."

I'd been going to mom's appointments with my dad and was the note-taker. I wrote down everything that was said but rarely spoke, myself. That started to change. I told the physician that mom was doing worse; she had a hard time with stairs, was almost too weak to stand, and couldn't entertain the idea of food. "But her tumors are shrinking," was her reply.

The next day, mom took a fall at home. Dad called an ambulance and I met them in the Emergency Department. While they were moving her up to an inpatient room, I pulled my dad aside and told him I wanted to involve another physician in mom's case. He looked stunned. "Why would you do that?"

"Dad," I said, "I know she says the tumors are shrinking, but that's all she's looking at. She's not looking at mom. Have you ever seen her this sick? I want the tumors to shrink, too, but not if we kill her in the process."

"Will she be offended if we tell her we want to see a different doctor?" He was worried about hurting this physician's feelings. He had seen a genuine friendship grow between his wife and her oncologist and was worried she'd be upset if we sought out another opinion. I tried to reassure him that doctors experience this kind of thing all the time and don't take it personally. I wasn't as interested in being factual as I was getting another set of eyes on her. Not her tumors, not her white blood count, her.

He took a minute to think about it. He knew mom wouldn't be happy seeing a different doctor, but agreed that maybe there was another treatment out there that wouldn't be so hard on her.

I never got the chance to make that call. When I went to work the next morning, I looked up the phone numbers of two of my favorite oncologists but before I could dial, I got a call. "Come to the hospital now. Mom took a turn last night." She was gone two days later.

When I reflect on it now, I keep coming back to the same thing: treat the person, not just the disease. I have no doubt that my mom's oncologist was a competent physician, or that she wanted my mom to recover, or that she did the very best she knew to do. But it has to be more than disease management. We have to notice how these treatments are affecting patients, their lives, their well-being, even their families.

If you're a physician, ask yourself: do you treat illness or do you treat people?

THE "PITY" LOOK

When I lived in the midwest, I belonged to a church that had some really wonderful people in it. People who genuinely cared about each other and would step up and help whenever someone was in need. When someone's spouse was hospitalized, people delivered meals. If someone needed childcare, there was a list of vetted teenagers up for the job. When you needed someone to talk to, there were people who didn't offer advice, just a good listening ear and a shoulder to cry on. It was really a nice thing to belong to.

There were a few people there, however, who had the very best of intentions but didn't really know what was helpful and what was actually making it worse. I remember when my mom was dying, people would come up to me and give me a look that I'm sure they thought was one of compassion and caring – forehead scrunched, eyes a little squinted, mouth turned down – but to me, it was a pity look. It said, "Oh dear, how awful. I'm so glad I'm not going through that." Nothing about that look says 'compassion' to me. Only pity.

And it really pulled the rug out from under me. I was trying hard to stay strong and accept that this was happening but as soon as I got that look, I felt like it was really something awful. Make no mistake, losing my mom was awful, but it seemed the natural order of things that I would likely outlive her, so I was trying to not treat it like it was the worst possible thing in the world to have happen. Getting that look made me feel like it was and it robbed me of my strength.

I think, in hospitals, we give patients that look a lot. And they recognize it. When we look right through the person and only see the illness, they know. When we are so concerned with making it seem like we really care but we don't, when we try to convince people that are concerned about them but we're not, we give a 'pity' look. A look we are consciously creating in order to look convincing. When we're more focused on ourselves and how we're coming across, they can feel it.

I've spent nearly my entire adult career listening to other people's troubles and I've learned that when I'm in my own head, trying to give the other person the impression that I'm really compassionate, I'm not present. I'm not doing them a service at all. When I finally stopped trying to manufacture a look that conveyed compassion and actually started *feeling* compassion, the look took care of itself. And people responded better to me.

I'm sure it was Brené Brown who said, "Compassion isn't feeling sorry for someone. It's honoring that person and what they're going through." So true.

When we look at someone with pity, we send a message that we are so grateful we're not going through what they're going through. We send a message that what they're dealing with is awful, and when they're trying hard to rise above and push through, a look of pity can knock them back a few steps.

If you're not sure what to do with your face, try mirroring the other person. Better yet, don't focus on your face. Focus on being present for them. Listen. Reflect. Say what you see. Please don't make the 'pity' face.

SILENCE AND PRESENCE MAY BE ALL YOU NEED

I saw a video a couple of weeks ago from one of my very favorite authors, Brené Brown. She was talking about sympathy and empathy and something she said really stuck with me. "When someone shares something really painful, maybe the best response is, 'I don't even know what to say right now, I'm just so glad you told me.' Because the truth is, rarely can a response make something better. What makes something better is connection."

I've been in many painful situations and some of my worst memories aren't of the situation itself, but of the thoughtless things well-meaning people say when they think they're being helpful. "Don't worry, there's a light at the end of the tunnel." "God doesn't give you any more than you can handle." "You're strong, you can get through this." "You think this is bad, I know someone who has it way worse than you." People can say some incredibly idiotic things when they're trying to help but I tend to cut them some slack because I know they don't know any better.

For many of us, the more difficult situation is the one in which we are with someone who is suffering and we don't know what to say.

We struggle for just the right words that will make that person feel better. We can't take the uncomfortable silence so we say something, anything, hoping it'll be better than nothing.

The truth is, just simply being with another person can make all the difference.

When a person is suffering, he or she feels alone. It's not the kind of alone like 'no one understands what I'm going through or how I'm feeling.' The truth is, no two painful events are the same and no one can truly know how you feel, whether they've been through it or not. It's the kind of alone like 'no one wants to walk with me while I go through this.'

Simply having someone next to you, to hold your hand, sit with you, just be there… that's one of the most meaningful gifts you can give a person. Don't worry about what to say. Just show up.

THE DOCTOR-PATIENT RELATIONSHIP

The relationship you have with your primary care physician can mean the difference between life and death.

How's that for an opening statement?

My parents had my eldest brother, Chris, then 14 months later had my other brother, Andrew, and 18 months later had my sister, Mary. It was just the three of them in this tight cluster until 7 years later when I came along. Those two boys were full of energy, into everything, and went non-stop all day. She, on the other hand, was an introverted sensitive soul.

She also had a weight problem. For as long as I could remember she was extremely self-conscious about it. My brothers were skinny, especially Chris, and poor Mary got picked on. A lot.

It didn't help that our primary care physician was a scary looking old man who spoke in a thick German accent and used to tease her about her weight every year at her annual school physical. She dreaded those visits and, even as an adult, hated going to the doctor for fear that they'd say something unkind.

Those early pediatrician visits made a big impression on her. She thought every doctor was an old man who said things like, "Vell younk lady, you ah putting on some veight, again, yah? You haff to shtop eating so many cookies." And always in front of my brothers, giving them plenty of ammunition for teasing.

She never got over it. This was a woman who, in her late 30s, refused to go to a doctor when she clearly and unmistakably had gallstones. Incredibly painful gallstones which she insisted on treating with over the counter tylenol. They either resolved on their own or she just adjusted her pain tolerance, I'm not sure which. But it infuriated my mom who was a nurse, and me who worked at a hospital. We begged her to go to a doctor but she absolutely refused. She told us didn't want to go because she was sure they'd get on her case about her weight. Exasperated, Mom and I finally gave up.

Fast forward to the fall of 2012. Mary was suffering from some insanely horrible back pain. Nothing over the counter could touch it. She'd gone to a chiropractor, a massage therapist, and an acupuncturist, but got no relief at all. I remember her telling me that driving over railroad tracks made her see stars.

Finally, I said, "That's it. I'm getting you an appointment to see a doctor. We have GOT to get this looked at." A few days later, I was able to get her in to see an internal medicine physician with the medical group I worked with. Although I turned my head when he asked her to take her shirt off, there was no way not to notice the giant lump she had on her breast. It was huge. Softball size huge. I couldn't believe my eyes.

A few imaging tests later and it was confirmed. The pain in her back wasn't a bulging disc or muscle spasms. It was stage 4 breast cancer with compression fractures in her spine. The cancer had spread from her breast, through her rib cage and into her back. There was nothing they could do. They gave her six months. And they were right.

I was as supportive as I knew how to be but I had to ask why she didn't go see a doctor as soon as she found the lump. It all came down to her fear of ridicule. She truly thought that her doctor would spend more time chastising her about her weight than addressing the lump in her breast.

Now I'm not going to blame my sister's death on her childhood physician; at some point, we all have to grow up and do the right thing. But she was truly traumatized as a little kid and those scars stayed with her well into adulthood.

Sometimes we say things and we don't mean anything by it. We're joking, we're trying to inject humor in an uncomfortable situation, or we're just not thinking about how the other person is hearing it. Whatever the reason – it matters.

Doctors, believe me, we listen to what you say to us. It may be a throwaway comment to you, but it's gospel to us. Venn you vant to make a shatement about your patient's veight, pause. Think about how that may impact their future decisions about seeking medical care.

I loved my old PCP. There was nothing he could have advised me to do that I wouldn't have done. And not because it was good advice; other doctors gave me the same advice, it was because I liked him. Liking him made me much more inclined to do what he asked. When he addressed issues about my weight, it was always with compassion and sensitivity

Doctors, you're more than just the treating physician. Inspiring behavioral change doesn't really happen without relationship. Get to know your patients. Be kind when you have to deliver some unpopular or sensitive news like needing to lose weight. The words you choose can make all the difference.

REACH OUT AND (VIRTUALLY) TOUCH SOMEONE

It's been a month and a half and we are, for the most part, still sheltering in place and working remotely. There are those who have grown weary of the restrictions and are anxious to get outside and back to work; I'm observing fewer people wearing masks and keeping a six foot distance from others, but most experts agree it's still too soon to open everything back up.

I'm concerned for those who are truly struggling; whether it's because of isolation or working in intense conditions caring for the sick. COVID-19 is taking its toll on us, emotionally and physically, and many of us are running out of coping mechanisms.

Which is why it was such a wonderful surprise to get a message from a friend I had in junior high. She and I didn't go to the same elementary school and we ended up in different high schools, but for two years in Emerson Junior High, she and I were inseparable.

We'd kept in touch over the years through various social media channels and even met for lunch several years ago, but hadn't actually spoken for quite some time. Then, out of nowhere, she sent a message asking if I wanted to do a video call and catch up.

It was wonderful.

It was so wonderful, in fact, that it prompted me to reach out to friends I see fairly regularly (or used to, before all this started) and set up video calls with them, too. I'm calling my brothers more often than I did and am much more active on sites like Facebook to keep in touch.

And this is significant because I'm not a person who generally craves a lot of social interaction. I love my alone time and need some peace and quiet in order to recharge. But this pandemic has made me realize that, when all is said and done, I'm not going to look back on my life wishing I'd spent *less* time with my family and friends.

Our patients, their families, and our staff are no different.

When trying to provide the very best experience, nothing beats a personal connection: someone reaching out to you, asking how you are, what they can do to help, and offering a shoulder to lean on.

It isn't always our clinical and technical expertise that makes an impression on people, but the way in which we interact with them that they remember. Taking a moment to reach out with genuine concern, actively listening, and giving people a non judgemental space to talk can make a world of difference. Even after 30 years.

IT'S BEEN TWENTY YEARS...

It was Christmas in a pandemic.

With no big family gatherings or plans with friends, this past Christmas was the first time I'd ever watched It's a Wonderful Life from start to finish without interruption. I've seen the film, but always in bits and pieces here and there, never all at once. I really enjoyed it and it stayed with me for several days afterwards. I kept thinking about the life of George Bailey and all he did and I wondered how many of us could relate. I mean, I've never pulled someone out of a hole in the ice and saved their life. How many of us have? We hear stories of people pulling others out of burning buildings or out of the way of a speeding car, but how many of us have actually done it? I started to wonder, "Are there any people alive today because of me? Have I really made a difference in the world?"

That was my thought one January evening as I was heading home and it occurred to me that maybe I could take credit for at least one person being alive.

I thought about my days in the mid-90s and early 2000s, working in organ donation and transplant, speaking with the families of patients who had just been declared brain dead and offering them the option to donate the organs. I know there were people whose lives were saved because of the generosity of those families. But would that have happened without me? The answer is probably yes. There might, and I mean *might*, have been a family that only agreed because of how they connected with me. Maybe.

So that would have to be good enough. Not quite as dramatic as pulling my brother out of the ice, but it would do.

Now here's where my story gets weird.

The very next day, I got a message on Facebook from someone I wasn't connected to, trying to send me a private message. I recognized his name immediately and accepted the friend request. It was a man I had met at a suburban Chicago hospital many years ago. His message was short, "Hi Kate – it's been such a long time – just wanted to reach out to you and say hi – (my wife) and I will never forget you – it's been 20 years since (my daughter) is gone – God Bless – "

I nearly fell out of my chair.

And then it hit me. Does your impact on this Earth depend on those big dramatic moments or can you make just as big an impression in those tiny acts of human kindness? The simple act of being present, of staying out of judgement, of listening, of helping someone who is going through an unbelievably difficult experience… this is how we make a difference in the world. Twenty years later and this family still remembered me. Remembered me enough to want to reach out and tell me.

This is what it means to work in healthcare. This is why I lead patient experience in healthcare systems. This is why I tell nurses, and food service workers, and housekeepers, and physicians, and registration teams, and telephone operators, and valet parkers, and security guards, and hospital presidents that how they treat people matters.

We have no idea what our patients and their families are going through when we see them. We only know they're scared, sad, sick and coming to us for help. How can we be anything but kind to them?

After 20 years, the kindness you showed someone will still be remembered and appreciated. Those people may not reach out over Facebook but they'll still be grateful to you. You're their George Bailey. And you absolutely made a difference in the world.

IT'S NOT JUST ANOTHER SCREENING TEST TO ME

Every six months I have some kind of test on my breasts. Every summer, it's a mammogram; every winter, it's an MRI.

While cancer runs in some families, it gallops in mine. There are only two relatives I know of who died of something other than cancer, and one of them really shouldn't count. My maternal grandfather was born premature and his heart wasn't quite ready to go. He had heart problems his whole life and died of a heart attack, so I don't think it's fair to include him in the mix.

In fact, my father had three different kinds of cancer. Not cancers that started in one place and metastasized to another, but three different primary tumors. Very unusual. So I think he should count as three.

When every female relative of yours dies of breast cancer, you start to think it may just be a foregone conclusion. As much as I try to keep a positive attitude, I don't really wonder *if* it's going to happen, but *when*.

So when it came time for my latest breast MRI, I was once again filled with the same familiar mix of anxiety and dread. Just six months earlier, my mammogram became an ultrasound that became a biopsy. It turned out to be nothing, but it scared the daylights out of me.

I was mentally preparing for something like that to happen again and reminding myself that whatever they find, they will have found it early. Early is good. Early is something none of my other relatives had.

I always wonder when I go in for these tests if the people at the front desk or the techs running the machines have any idea what's going on inside the patients' heads. To them, it's just another routine screening, but to me, it's something much more.

Every time I go in, I think of my maternal grandmother, my mom and my sister. I watched breast cancer metastasize to brain cancer in my grandma. At the end, she thought she was a kid again, back on her farm in Iowa, and she didn't know me at all. I was so mad at God for not letting her go out a little more gracefully.

I watched breast cancer metastasize to liver cancer in my mom. She went through some horrible treatments to shrink the tumors but they wreaked havoc on the rest of her. She got weaker and weaker until she couldn't even walk and died in the one place an RN of over 50 years doesn't want to die: a hospital.

I watched breast cancer take my sister just six months after her diagnosis. She thought she was merely experiencing really bad back pain but it was actually compression fractures from the cancer eating away at her spine. As an unmarried woman who had no insurance, she needed someone to navigate the healthcare system for her, and

I, as her only sister, did just that. She, at least, had the ending she wanted, on her terms. But it was still an ending.

So when I go in for these tests every six months, they aren't just routine maintenance for me. They are a reminder of how devastating this disease is, not only for the patients, but for those who love and care for them. I am terrified every six months. It hasn't gotten any easier.

And I'm on high alert for service failures. I am extra-sensitive to how I'm spoken to, how things are explained, the tone of voice they're using with me, the degree of kindness and gentleness they show, all of it.

This was a place I'd not been to before and I didn't know what to expect from them. I'm very happy to report they did a wonderful job. Although they couldn't possibly know what was going through my head or how anxious I was, they did a great job of caring for me from the moment I walked in to the moment I walked out.

If you're working in imaging, please keep this in mind. For you, it's just another day at the office. For the rest of us, it's something much, much more.

CARE FOR OTHERS BY CARING FOR YOURSELF

Years ago when I was working in organ donation and transplant, I fell apart one night on my way to a case. I was leading the Family Support Services department and part of my job was to approach family members in the hospital after they'd gotten the news that their loved one had died and ask them if they'd be willing to donate organs for patients on the transplant waiting list.

As difficult as this kind of work can be, it was incredible to see the good that came of such a selfless decision. Upon receiving the worst news imaginable, families were able to look outside their situation and think of helping others. Where they once were lost in grief, they now had hope knowing that their loved one would save others.

It had been a particularly busy month and I had been on several cases involving children. I was at home that evening trying to relax when my pager went off, telling me I needed to head to a level one trauma center about 20 miles away. There was a four-year-old who was likely going to be pronounced brain dead that evening and I needed to be there to talk with the family.

BETTER THAN I FOUND IT

I got in my car and started driving. Just before I got on the highway, I started to shake. First my hands, then my legs, then my whole body. I could feel my heart pounding and I was getting short of breath. I pulled over, looked around and didn't know where I was. I'd been on that road hundreds of times but nothing looked familiar. I felt completely lost, in a panic, not able to breathe.

I called the referral center, the ones who had dispatched me to this case, and when I heard the voice of my favorite coordinator on the other end of the line, I burst into tears. All I could say was, "No more kids, no more kids." He could barely understand me through the tears and gasps for air but after a few minutes he was able to calm me down.

They contacted the next person in the call schedule to go out and handle this case and had a colleague meet me at a local diner to talk to me about what had just happened. After several hours, many cups of decaf coffee and some ice cream, I realized I'd had a panic attack. The busy schedule, the intensity of the work, and the pressure of managing the department had caught up with me. I'd never had anything like that happen to me before and, thankfully, I learned how to never let it happen again.

1. **Find time for yourself.** There will always be pressure, deadlines, and stressors. Taking as little as five minutes out of the day to be quiet and still can do wonders for your mental health. Five minutes. Quiet. Breathe. Don't think about anything but your breath coming in and going out.

2. **Reach out**. We're not here to go it alone and do everything ourselves. Ask people for help. There's no shame in admitting we can't do it all. If that's your company culture, you're in the wrong company.

3. **Have a confidant**. Sometimes, just talking to someone you trust about what's going on can relieve a whole bunch of built up steam. Saying it out loud takes away its power. Having a trusted friend who listens and supports you doesn't change the situation, but can make it easier to face.

4. **Lay off the booze**. Instead of flopping down on the couch after work and pouring yourself a drink or three, try a brisk walk around the block. As difficult as it is to convince me to start moving, I'm always glad once I do. It's one thing to intellectually know the benefits of exercise, it's quite another to experience them.

5. **Use your vacation days**. They're good for you. Go away for a while. Don't check your work email. Unplug from work and focus on you.

6. **Re-evaluate your purpose**. Maybe part of the reason you're feeling stressed is because this isn't the right job for you. There are so many people out there killing themselves for a job they don't even like. If this really isn't your thing, your body and mind might be trying to tell you so.

As much as I truly loved my work there, I left a few months later. I knew I had done some wonderful work and helped a lot of people, but felt it was time to move on. And it was okay.

There have been times since then where I've felt stressed, over-worked and under a lot of pressure, but these 6 simple steps have staved off another panic attack.

What do *you* do to stay calm when things get to be too much?

TELL ME AGAIN WHAT IT IS YOU DO?

It's funny trying to explain to people what I do for a living.

I get a lot of blank stares, puzzled looks, and plenty of people who ask if I'm the smile police (I love that one). But mostly, people think I'm the complaint department. And I am to some degree. Complaints and grievances are a big part of the job, to be sure. But there's so much more to it than that.

In several hospitals at which I've worked, there's a patient relations team and a patient experience team. The patient relations team handles complaints like poor service, lost belongings, and mis-communication. They do the internal investigation, follow up with patients, and resolve the grievances within 30 days. There is always more than enough to keep them busy. The patient experience team, on the other hand, is there to change the culture with the hope of one day making the patient relations team obsolete.

The experience team puts together the Standards of Behavior for the entire organization. They overhaul new employee orientation to be primarily about service. They do one-on-one coaching for staff and physicians. They create and lead a Patient and Family Advisory Council. They look at all the shiny new technology aimed at improving patient satisfaction and make recommendations about which ones to invest in and which ones to avoid. They integrate with the quality department and help staff understand how the two are connected. They analyze the survey data and devise plans for improvement. And they take the heat if scores don't go up.

Culture change is hard. It takes a really long time and yet so many executive teams don't have an appetite for that. They're largely results-driven and want to see the numbers move right away. I don't blame them, but that's really not how it works. I once had a CEO who wanted daily patient experience scores on his desk every morning. Daily. I obliged, but told him I wasn't going to take any action on daily scores, only the things we saw as trends over time. Needless to say, I didn't last too long there.

But it gets back to what I do for a living. The short answer is, "I create systems in healthcare designed to provide the very best in service excellence." That includes a lot of things, most of them proactive rather than reactive.

When the systems are designed well, the right people are in place, and they have the tools and support they need, great things happen. That's what I do for a living.